Implementing ISO 9001:2015

A practical guide to busting myths surrounding quality management systems

Implementing ISO 9001:2015

A practical guide to busting myths surrounding quality management systems

ANDREW W NICHOLS

IT Governance Publishing

IT Governance Publishing Ltd
Unit 3, Clive Court
Bartholomew's Walk
Cambridgeshire Business Park
Ely, Cambridgeshire
CB7 4EA
United Kingdom
www.itgovernancepublishing.co.uk

Formerly published as *Exploding the Myths Surrounding ISO9000 – A practical implementation guide* in 2013 by IT Governance Publishing.

This edition published in the United Kingdom in 2022 by IT Governance Publishing.

ISBN 978-1-78778-374-4

FOREWORD

The international standard ISO 9000 has been adopted by organizations in more than 170 countries and is the biggest-selling ISO standard since the International Organization for Standardization was formed in 1947. In 30 or more years of use by a wide variety of organizations, much has been said and written about the three documents, collectively known as ISO 9000: ISO 9000, ISO 9001, and ISO 9004. With the publication of the most recent version, ISO 9001:2015, came additional guidance in the form of the document ISO/TC 9002. ISO 9000 is important as it is what is called a "normative reference" and contains definitions, ISO 9004 is guidance on the sustainability of an effective quality management system (QMS), and a guidance document, ISO/TS 9002, was published shortly after. Sadly, few users reference these valuable documents in seeking answers for 'what' or 'how to' questions.

Although a great deal of ISO 9001 would appear, at first reading, to be 'common sense,' a significant number of myths have been promulgated, often from confusing what ISO specifically requires compared to that which is commonly implemented, and what is frequently found to be acceptable to pass third-party certification audits.

Based on earlier versions of the ISO 9001 requirements (there have been four previous editions), these myths have misled implementers, delayed or even prevented an organization's adoption of the requirements, and may have also delayed managements' understanding of the use of ISO 9001 as a tool for control and improvement of business processes.

This book, then, is an attempt to expose many of the myths and enable a better understanding of ISO 9001:2015 by those who seek to create, implement, and improve an effective QMS for their organization.

PREFACE

Universally known as ISO 9000, the international standard for QMSs continues to have a significant effect on organizations around the world. After more than 30 years of experience by user organizations, auditors, consultants, and trainers, there are fundamental misunderstandings of what is involved in applying the requirements in ISO 9001, particularly with the most recent revision, published in 2015. This is in part due to the adoption, by the writing committee, of the concept of 'risk-based thinking.' More on this later.

ISO 9001 was intended for use as a 'voluntary' basis for agreement on quality assurance between customers and their suppliers, and in the early 1990s third-party certification, which independently audited and confirmed compliance, became a popular option for both parties. Customers saw a cost-effective alternative to maintaining supplier quality departments, instead relying on the certification bodies to maintain compliance of their suppliers' QMSs. In some respects, it is this certification that has fueled several of the myths surrounding ISO 9001.

Major purchasing organizations often require ISO certification as a prerequisite for those wanting to do business as a supplier; however, they rarely provided practical assistance with implementation to those suppliers. Further, the ISO 9000 guidance documents were never designed to be a roadmap for implementation, focusing more on improvement than the basics of creating and implementing a QMS approach to an organization's creation and delivery of products and services.

Preface

Early adopters of ISO 9001 – particularly in the US – coined the phrase, *"Say what you do, do what you say and prove it"* as a description of what implementing a QMS involved. This may have been appropriate to passing a certification audit in the 1990s, but is a long way short of what is involved with effective implementation of and compliance with today's ISO 9001 requirements. Indeed, ISO 9001:2015 was specifically designed to align with the needs of an organization's methods of conducting business and gives freedom to those implementing the QMS by being less prescriptive.

At the time of writing, there have been seven years of implementation of the latest version of the requirements, either by organizations that have upgraded from an ISO 9001:2008-compliant/certified QMS or for those new to this experience. As has happened since the original publication in 1987, myths have become common. Many originated when the committee draft standards (CD-1, CD-2) were circulated for comment and leaked to a wider audience than was originally intended, who were eager to know what the revised standard included.

Taken out of context, many requirements suddenly gained 'myth' status, even before the 2015 version was formally published. Here, then, are the ISO 9001:2015 requirements and some of the common myths affecting them, along with practical, experience-based advice, including top tips applicable to implementing a specific requirement.

ABOUT THE AUTHOR

Andrew (Andy) W Nichols, CQP FCQI, has more than 30 years' experience of management systems. As the quality manager of a UK-based NATO contractor, he was responsible for developing a quality assurance program to meet the AQAP 1 Quality Assurance requirements, when supplying communications equipment (hardware and software) to the SHAPE organization. Subsequently, as design/supplier assurance manager for a well-known British-based metrology equipment company, he was on the leadership team responsible for achieving ISO 9001:1987 certification – a first in class.

In 1990, Andy joined the first UK accredited certification body (LRQA) as a lead assessor, quickly becoming a supervisor and trainer, responsible for mentoring new certification auditors, leading internal sales training, and conducting ISO 9000-based training for clients. He performed some of the earliest ISO 9000 certification audits in the US. In 1992, Andy joined a small team responsible for opening the LRQA North American operations.

Shortly after arriving in the US, he pursued a career as a consultant and trainer with Excel Partnership Inc, a leading provider of QMS implementation support. He delivered hundreds of ISO 9000 training courses, covering implementation, documentation, and auditing, making the material relevant to audiences ranging from shop floor personnel to CEOs of Fortune 500 companies.

As an instructional designer, Andy led, and contributed to, the development of best-in-class training courses for ISO

9001, ISO 14001, ISO/IEC 17024, QS-9000, ISO/TS 16949, and ISO/IEC 17025.

His clients included Tellabs, Chrysler, GKN, General Motors, Visteon, Hyundai Motor Manufacturing of America, Hewlett-Packard, Dresser Industries, ANSI, the USDA, and many branches of the U.S. Department of Defense.

Andy has held certifications with the International Register of Certificated Auditors (IRCA) and the RABQSA (now Exemplar Global) as a lead auditor of QMSs. He is a fellow of the UK's Chartered Quality Institute and has been a member of the American Society for Quality (ASQ).

Andy joined the global certification body NQA as its East Coast sales manager in 2008 and contributed to its overall sales success.

In September 2016, Andy joined the Michigan Manufacturing Technology Center, a Top 5 NIST Manufacturing Extension Partner in the US. As a quality program manager, he brings his 40 years of industrial expertise to clients seeking to improve their manufacturing operations and has led clients through successful transitions (based on ISO 9001:2008) and 'ground up' implementations where no formal quality system existed. He has led a significant number of clients through ISO 9001:2015, as well as AS9100D and IATF 16949 implementations. He also guides clients in sales management and information security management systems to ISO/IEC 27001.

Andy is a regular technical contributor to online forums, LinkedIn groups, and blogs.

ACKNOWLEDGMENTS

The many professionals I've met during my career, for providing me with the opportunities to learn from their experiences. I also appreciate the clients I've had the pleasure of assisting when they implemented the requirements of ISO 9001:2015, including the aerospace version, AS9100D, and automotive supplier requirements IATF 16949.

C Allen Powell – mentor, friend, and architect of the 5 Phase Implementation model.

David Middleton, for giving me the opportunity to pursue a successful career as a trainer and consultant.

Jeff Monk, who trained me as a lead auditor. Jeff wrote one of the very first recognized lead auditor courses.

The Deming Institute for permission to reproduce Dr. Deming's 14 Points.

John Owen, IAF Secretariat, for permission to reproduce IAF documents.

Charles Corrie, ISO TC 176 SC2 Secretary, for permission to reproduce ISO documents or parts thereof.

The management team at the Michigan Manufacturing Technology Center: Mike Coast, Bob Lyscas, and Charlie Westra. ITGP manuscript reviewer, Alan Field, for his helpful comments during the production of this book.

CONTENTS

INTRODUCTION

In September 2015, the much-anticipated sixth version of ISO 9001 was published, and, with it, several myths were given life. Implementations of QMSs, based on the requirements of ISO 9001, have been plagued by misunderstood and misinterpreted requirements, from the earliest version back in 1987. New myths have arrived with the publication of the ISO 9001:2015 edition. With the publication of the requirements normally preceding any formal guidance document, such as ISO 9004 or the new ISO/TC 9002, the lack of anything other than the normative reference has given rise to a good deal of speculation about what is intended to be included in an organization's QMS.

It has become common practice to reference some of the many online forums and groups where users can solicit answers to questions regarding the interpretations of the ISO 9001 requirements or what will be acceptable to a third-party auditor, aiding their certification. As with many things found on the Internet, much of what is opined in such forums is apocryphal, based on just a few implementation experiences or (certification) audit experiences.

CHAPTER 1: ISO 9001 REQUIREMENTS, MYTHS, AND GUIDANCE

In this chapter, we look in-depth at the requirements of ISO 9001:2015, including some of the more common myths associated with each requirement and guidance based on more than 6 years of implementation in more than 50 organizations. A copy of the ISO 9000, and ISO/TS 9002 standards should be obtained to gain the best understanding of ISO 9001.

At the time of writing, ISO 9004 is being considered for updating as a requirements document to complement ISO 9001, so comments regarding that guidance are not included. Readers may wish to visit the ISO website for the latest details. More on these guidance documents later.

Some of the myths may have originated around the earlier versions and are commonly applied to the 2015 version of ISO 9001, so have been included here for those readers coming to ISO implementation for the first time.

ISO 9001 has five key sections:

1. Introduction
2. Scope
3. Normative References
4. Terms and Definitions
5. Quality Management Systems – Requirements

Rarely are all the texts of this 27-page document ever fully read and completely understood. Instead, most readers tend to focus on the section 4 requirements, mainly because that is where the requirements for a QMS are specified. It is these requirements, plus the desire by an organization to be certified, which draw attention away from key information found in sections 1 through 3! Sadly, this is a little like children being taught to recite multiplication tables without knowing the mathematical purpose.

History has shown us that, typically, quality management activities in an organization were frequently performed to meet customer requirements – often through compliance with a contractual obligation. Customers flow down their supplier quality assurance requirements or require a supplier to be ISO 9001:2015 certified as a basis of doing business with them. No doubt many readers will be seeking information on ISO 9001 for that very purpose. This is still true today, however, if we adopt the popular maxim of Dr. Deming: *"Quality is everyone's responsibility."* Clearly the quality system should be embedded in the organization's everyday operations and functions, and not seen as an 'appendage' to the core of that organization.

It was only with ISO 9001:2000 that any thought was really given to providing, in the document itself, a description of how all the requirements of the Standard were supposed to come together – as the basis of the organization's QMS.

This situation, where users simply refer to only the section 4 requirements, exists despite volumes of guidance being published by the ISO technical committees and a significant number of books on implementing and auditing ISO 9001! Not spending time to grasp the whole document may delay the fullest understanding of its application. Following a major online survey of users in 2014, the technical committees responsible for the creation of the ISO 9000 standards have attempted to make the requirements align better with the needs of an organization to help make the QMS integral to the organization's business processes.

Now entering the sixth year of publication and with another user survey being closed in December 2020, it has been decided that there will be no revisions to the 2015 requirements – this should see users through to 2025 without any changes being necessary to their QMSs.

Top tip

Obtain copies of ISO 9000, ISO 9001, and ISO/TS 9002 to study. Along with the guidance here, you'll be off to a good start.

Introduction

The introduction to ISO 9001 talks about the adoption of a QMS as being a strategic decision and to help improve overall performance and as a basis for sustainable development initiatives. It lists the potential benefits of implementing a QMS based on the requirements of the Standard:

- Consistently supplying products and services that meet applicable requirements (customer, regulatory, etc.)
- Opportunities to enhance customer satisfaction
- Addressing risks and opportunities associated with the organization's context and objectives

- Demonstrating conformity (this would include third-party certification)
- It further states that the Standard doesn't imply any type of formal approach to risk management

It is interesting to note that the word 'risk' is introduced – but then mentioned only a few times in the requirements sections 4 through 10. Perhaps controversially, many quality professionals will offer opinions that the concept of risk was always embedded in the application of ISO 9001 – now it is clearly stated.

Quality management principles are described in section 0.2 of the Introduction, including:

- Customer focus
- Leadership
- Engagement of people
- Process approach
- Improvement
- Evidence-based decision making
- Relationship management

Despite being mentioned in the Introduction and throughout the various requirements sections, the description refers the reader to ISO 9000 2.3 for further explanations of each.

The "Process Approach" is section 0.3 of the Introduction, which describes several concepts that are supposed to be incorporated in the organization's approach to quality management – a system of interlinked and interacting processes. A diagram, on page viii of ISO 9001 (figure 1), shows elements of a single process in terms of:

- Sources of inputs (predecessor processes)

- Inputs (energy, matter, information)
- Activities
- Outputs (energy, matter, information)
- Receivers of inputs (subsequent processes)

Also shown are possible control points for measurement and monitoring (specifically at input and output).

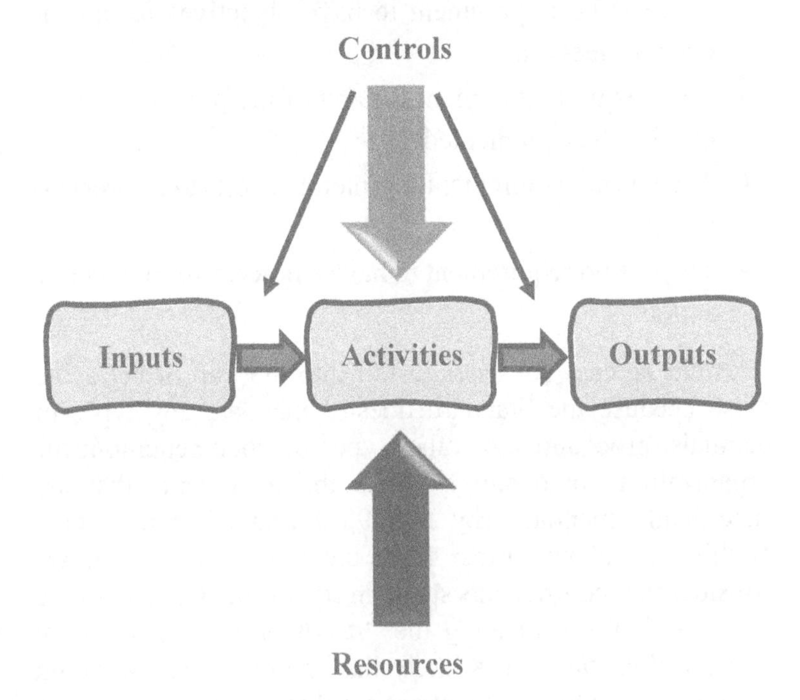

Figure 1: Elements of a process

It is worth remembering that some key features which should have caused the conventional wisdoms of previous versions of ISO 9001 to be laid to rest have, instead, created more mythology.

These include the following:

- There is no required quality manual. Only the scope of the QMS, quality objectives, and quality policy are required to be documented.
- There is no requirement for a formal approach to risk management – it even states this in Annex A.4 "Risk-based thinking".
- There is no requirement to have objectives for all the QMS processes.
- There is no requirement for any of the processes of the QMS to be documented.
- There is no requirement for internal audits to be process-based.
- There is no requirement to have a process for preventive action.

It would be easy for users to fall into the trap of believing these because the Standard doesn't mandate any types of manuals, procedures, or other types of documentation; the organization could simply write the documents that are specifically mandated by ISO 9001 and leave it at that. Nothing could be further from the truth, however, if we consider the requirements stated in section 4, "Context of the Organization"; in meeting the *"needs and expectations of interested parties,"* it is likely that the organization would identify a need to document certain things for:

- Training purposes
- Knowledge retention
- Governance or similar policy
- Meeting customers' expectations/requirements, or regulatory agencies' requirements

Indeed, it is difficult to conceive that improvements may be made to any process or related aspect without formally defining and documenting those things, so that improvements can be a) identified and b) implemented.

It is, as most readily understand, difficult to hit a moving target, and writing things down is a universally accepted place to start the improvement journey.

Another consideration of interested parties, especially customers and (if applicable) regulatory agencies, is that they may require the organization to document many of the plans, processes, responsibilities, authorities, controls, and actions necessary to assure the products had a good chance of being correct to the specification.

Top tips

Consider all the reasons the organization would create documentation of its QMS process, responsibilities, results, etc., and let that determine why and what forms the documentation. Engage all functions in the decision and the creation of documentation. People 'own' what they create.

Don't be overly concerned about what hierarchy of documentation is needed. Find a placeholder in relation to the processes: input, control, resource, or output.

Don't structure your organization's QMS around the requirements of ISO 9001.

QMSs: Requirements

Scope (1)

Before anyone leaps into implementing a QMS based upon the ISO 9001 requirements, it's highly recommended to read through the Scope at the very beginning – something which is often overlooked. The Scope section defines the conditions when an organization considers implementing a QMS, when it:

- Needs to demonstrate its ability to consistently provide products and services that meet customer and applicable regulatory requirements
- Aims to enhance customer satisfaction through the effective application of the system, including processes for improvement of the system and the assurance of conformity to customer and applicable statutory and regulatory requirements

It goes on to state that the requirements are generic and are intended to be applicable to any organization, regardless of its type or size, or the products and services it provides.

Myth Alert!

"My organization is too small to implement ISO 9001."

Myth Busted!

As can be seen from the scope, ISO 9001:2015 is intended to be implemented by all types of organizations, no matter how big or small. It can be a challenge for many "micro-organizations", (perhaps one, two, three or four people) to ensure some of the requirements of ISO 9001 are adequately implemented over time, especially aspects such as internal audits.

Top tip

Consider using an experienced, qualified professional on a part-time basis, to take care of some of the implementation aspects of ISO 9001. Tasks can include managing and reporting on the supplier relationships, internal audits, management reviews, liaison with external bodies such as calibration labs, certification bodies and their auditors and managing corrective actions and improvement opportunities.

Normative References (2)

Since the ISO 9001 standard is written to have the same meaning in many languages, it is important that words which represent key concepts on which a QMS are built have common definitions. Without a clear understanding of these key words, designing, implementing, and improving a QMS are not going to be as effective.

Discussions on Internet forums will quickly reveal how important it is to have a common understanding of terminology. One example, which we will explore in a later section, is defining competence. Online dictionaries show several definitions that may not fully address the intent, in the context of ISO 9001. This key definition isn't found in the Standard itself, however, but in ISO 9000, which is the "Normative Reference." It contains the terms and definitions necessary to guide the reader through the ISO 9001 requirements.

Competence, which is the subject of section 7.2 of ISO 9001, is defined in the vocabulary document – ISO 9000 (3.10.4) – as the *"ability to apply knowledge and skills to achieve intended results."*

In considering the requirements specified, it is easier to see that once competencies have been defined (and demonstrated), some actions may be necessary, including training, to address any shortfalls identified. Such a process will, now a better understanding has been gained, lead to time and money being saved, compared to conventional training programs in which a number of hours of training are required, regardless of any need being identified for an individual employee.

Top tips

Ensure that everyone involved in the creation of the QMS fully understands the terminology applicable to their process.

For example:

- ***Training*** isn't competency
- ***Calibration*** and ***verification*** aren't the same thing
- ***Inspection*** and ***audit*** are not synonymous
- ***Nonconformities*** don't require root-cause corrective action

- ***Calibration*** isn't a simple check of a gauge against another

Terms and Definitions (3)

ISO 9001 has employed the terminology of "product" as the resulting output from the QMS. The background to the development of ISO 9001 was, after all, the military hardware-oriented Defence Standards. From user feedback since 1987, it became obvious that organizations which provided services (often alongside their product) had struggled to implement the requirements of ISO 9001, although having a formal QMS was found to be useful and often a customer requirement. The need for less product-oriented terminology was called for.

Under this heading, a clear statement is made that where "product" is mentioned, users may substitute "service" if this is applicable to their needs. Also, a reference is made here to the use of ISO 9000 – the vocabulary document – for other definitions and how the terms used are linked. This is particularly useful to demystify some relationships, for example the roles of controlling non-conformance and the need for corrective actions, which are frequently lumped together with (financially) disastrous results! Oddly, many organizations balk at spending the US$250 or so, when that cost can easily be avoided by using the direction the vocabulary provides. Compare that to the cost of responding to a certification body audit report that identifies major nonconformities!

The Context of the Organization (4)

The inclusion of this requirement was intended by the technical committee to provide an 'anchor' or connection from the issues of running an organization to the development and implementation of a QMS. Historically, quality and management systems have been perceived as something that is additional or extra to the actual business of managing an organization. Indeed, the word 'quality' often means the responsibility for its management is offloaded onto a designated individual, usually a quality manager. Part of the Annex SL or high-level structure adopted across many of the management systems-related ISO standards (ISO 14001, ISO 27001, et al), the Clause 4 requirements are intended to direct the organization to look to the future – a sort of strategic planning, without calling it that.

For the first time in traditional QMS requirements, there has been an attempt to align the organization's quality system with its business operations in a manner that makes the resulting goals, processes, controls, measurements, and actions assist the overall success!

Sub-clause 4.1, "Understanding the organization and its context," includes the need to *"determine the external and internal issues that are relevant to its purpose and its strategic direction and that affect its ability to achieve the intended results of its Quality Management System."*

Reference is also made to the need to *"monitor and review information"* related to these issues.

Myth alert!

"These internal and external issues need to be addressed in a procedure."

Myth busted!

Internal and external issues can be simply addressed by an organization through the use of business analysis tools, such as SWOT (Strengths, Weaknesses, Opportunities and Threats) or PEST (Political, Economic, Social, and Technological). These are macro views of the organization and give an indication of issues affecting an organization. Using SWOT will help identify internal (strengths and weaknesses) and external (opportunities and threats) issues.

For example, at the time of writing, in the western industrial marketplace, a SWOT would confirm that a key strength of many organizations is their people, in the following terms:

- Experienced
- Tenured
- Knowledgeable
- Skilled
- Flexible
- Etc.

However, as with many strengths, they can also be viewed as a weakness. In this case, many of these experienced and skilled employees are facing retirement. This 'silver tsunami' will result in the potential loss of a significant amount of organizational knowledge. Due to a variety of factors, education systems and employers have not prepared people to enter the workplace with even basic skills that are transferable to the workplace. The 'risk' becomes how the organization will address this weakness since it will, inevitably, adversely affect the ability to deliver a quality product.

The question becomes, within the scope of the QMS, what to do about this risk?

The ISO 9001 requirement doesn't make it clear what is supposed to be done with this information. However, when considering the input to management review, it is clear that this information is the source of what would be reviewed and the results of addressing the weaknesses and threats, for example. More on this later, in section 6, "Planning".

Once the SWOT is performed, it makes sense to keep a watchful eye on its content because changes, over time, will affect the analysis.

The Standard goes on, in sub-clause 4.2, to require the organization to *"Understand the needs and expectations of interested parties."* Referencing ISO 9000, we can see that interested parties simply means stakeholders, i.e. the organization's owners, customers, employees, and suppliers, and, as applicable, regulatory agencies. It is a requirement for the organization to determine:

- *"The interested parties that are relevant to the Quality Management System and*
- *The requirements of these interested parties that are relevant to the Quality Management System."*

Once again, the need to monitor and review information about this is required.

One drawback of ISO 9001:2015 that can affect users is grasping how the requirements are intended to interrelate to form a true system. As we read through the sections, there are backwards references to previously stated requirements as a nod to their connectedness. Unfortunately, there are few (one?) forward-looking references and experience shows that the context of the organization requirements can be related to a key feature of an effective QMS – the "Management Review" requirement (9.3). As we will discuss later, there is no guidance within the Standard that points out this interrelationship to help readers understand how this system should function. Instead, they would have to purchase yet another ISO publication, in this case ISO/TS 9002 (which is a technical specification providing implementation guidance for ISO 9001), to obtain any information on such connectedness between clauses.

Top tips

A simple SWOT analysis is a good way to determine the internal and external issues. The organization's leadership should conduct this analysis and use the 'vital few' issues to create a strategic plan of action.

Unless it's not very obvious to the organization's leadership, there is no need to rank the risks, even in a simple manner such as 'high,' 'medium,' or 'low.'

The last part of the clause on the context of the organization deals with determining the scope of the QMS (4.3). As the word 'scope' suggests, an organization has some degree of flexibility to select what functions and activities, products and services fall within the 'focus' or the boundaries of the QMS – with some exceptions: If conformity to the ISO 9001 requirements is going to be claimed – let's say for the purpose of being certified by a third-party conformity assessment body (a registrar) – then the requirements cannot be claimed to be not applicable if they affect the organization's ability or responsibility to ensure conformity of products and services and customer satisfaction. In simple terms, if the organization creates new product design work, it cannot avoid compliance of the QMS with the 8.3 requirements – for any reason.

For example, if Apple were seeking ISO 9001 certification, it would not be able to claim that product design was inapplicable. Similarly, it cannot claim to manufacture, since – at the time of writing – manufacturing Apple products such as the iPhone, iPad and Apple Watch are carried out by contractors such as Foxconn Technology (the trading name of Taiwanese business Hon Hai Precision Industry Co., Ltd.). This may seem obvious at first sight, but the application of scope to a QMS is fraught with nuance and many rules.

In considering what is in and out of the scope of the QMS, the organization needs to consider the requirements above, relating to 4.1 Understanding the context and 4.2 Understanding the needs and expectations of interested parties.

The scope is required to be maintained as "documented information" – the first time this somewhat obtuse reference to any form of documentation is made. This terminology is referenced and discussed later. Typically, a scope statement might describe the products and services the organization offers to the marketplace, locations, and justification why some ISO 9001 requirements are not applicable – not performing product design is a classic example.

Examples include:

- "The design and manufacture of…"
- "The manufacture, maintenance, and servicing of…"
- "The distribution of…"
- "The management of technical engineering staff to…"

- "The installation, commissioning, service, and repair of..."

The product(s)/services are usually described, including other descriptions of specific industries served, materials used in the product, process types employed, etc., to give details to prospective buyers of the capabilities of the organization.

Turning to the final sub-clause of the first major requirement of ISO 9001, we see it relates to the QMS (4.4) and the processes that are included within it.

Myth alert!

"We'll use the diagram in the ISO standard as it shows how the QMS interacts."

Myth busted!

Although it might seem a very tempting proposition to fast-track the creation of a QMS by using the Plan-Do-Check-Act (PDCA)-based diagram (figure 2) on page viii of the ISO 9001 standard, it's not a model to describe the organization's QMS. What's shown is how the QMS is supposed to operate in support of the business, not how the business operates. For example, in organizations that design innovative products, it is this process that precedes any customer demand, through sales, etc. In another case, a business may contract with a customer to perform design.

The key is that the organization's leadership should determine how it wants the processes to operate in coordination to be most effective. Using what the ISO 9001 standard refers to as "The Process Approach," the organization can focus its efforts on understanding how product and information should flow from one function to another (see figure 1 on page viii of ISO 9001).

Top tips

Create a large-scale (high-level) process map that demonstrates how requirements are processed from the inputs to the resulting outputs.

Use existing documentation – in whatever format and media it exists – to populate the processes as inputs, controls, etc.

Show who does work involved in the processes, who has responsibility, and, most importantly, who has authority. Create what else may be needed to fill gaps. Document processes. Experience shows that a process can be described adequately in approximately nine steps. Identify where measurements and/or monitoring of product or information is required and what is needed for that.

Be careful NOT to create a system of documentation, instead of a documented system. Ensure that the inputs and outputs align – specifically those that occur internally. Experience shows it is these internal interfaces that do not allow information to flow through the organization. It shouldn't become an exercise in papering over the cracks that exist within the organization.

Section 4.4 (f) of ISO 9001 also mentions – for the first time in an ISO standard on quality management – the terms "risk and opportunity." It is this and a sprinkling of those words in other places in the Standard that have set people off to create a mountain out of what really should be viewed in simple terms.

Myth alert!

"We'll use a failure modes and effects analysis (FMEA) to document our risks."

"We need a risk register and to rank risks as high, medium, or low."

"We need to evaluate each process of the QMS for risks."

Myth busted!

The use of the quality tool FMEA is an obvious choice for inclusion as a way to show compliance with this section of ISO 9001. The correct terminology for the tool is Potential Failure Modes, Effects and Criticality Analysis (PFMECA) and has been around since the 1980s, being widely adopted – with mixed results – by the automotive industry.

FMEA is used within the overall new product development process (often called Advanced Product Quality Planning), which may be applied to the product design (DFMEA) and product manufacturing process(es) (PFMEA). A cross-functional team analyzes (in this case) process and identifies potential failures (modes) and then applies ranking criteria such as the severity (S) of the failure, the occurrence (O), and the ability to detect (D) the failure, should it occur. The product of these rankings, S x O x D = the risk priority number (RPN), which is where the connection to risk occurs. It appears that people immediately rush to the conclusion that the tool should be used to evaluate the QMS processes.

This would entail a considerable amount of work – and is not what the ISO TC 176 committees imagined would be necessary, hence the commentary in the Annex A4 texts "Risk-based thinking" clarifying that a formal risk management process is not a requirement.

This non-prescriptive approach eschews the need for the organization to document even the risks it has identified, let alone assigning a ranking method, or any form of risk treatment. Annex B of the ISO 9001 standard – which is an informative reference – lists the other ISO standards that may be of use to QMS implementers in setting up or improving that system. No reference is made to any guidelines pertaining to risk. In fact, it's the bibliography, tucked away on the last page (28), that includes ISO 31000 – the guidance on risk management and principles. None of the notes within ISO 9001 clauses refer to ISO 31000, so any thoughts about specific tools, lists, rankings, or applications of specific risk-based tools are NOT what is required.

Top tips

- Make a list of the interested parties and their needs/expectations. Record these in the management review records (9.3).
- Adopt a simple quality manual (see section 7.5) as a means to define a) the process, and their sequence and interaction as well as b) the scope of the QMS.
- Don't overcomplicate the analysis of risk by ranking the results of the SWOT, etc.

- Consider the use of process FMEA if, and only if, you want better control over your (manufacturing) processes.

Leadership (5)

Leadership and commitment are key to any initiative undertaken by the organization, if it is to be successful. The implementation of an ISO-based QMS is no different in that respect. Commitment comes, for the most part, from the leadership's active participation in the planning, creation, implementation, performance, and improvement of the QMS.

While it is – or should be – widely recognized that no implementation project is going to be successful without the active participation of the organization's leadership, including setting aside the necessary budgets, progress reviews, and so on, it is perhaps paradoxical that few myths exist around this role – that of leadership. Few nonconformities are found and reported relating to much, other than the failure of personnel to adequately respond to the audit question: "How do you affect the quality policy?" or "What is the quality policy, in your own words?" or some variation of this line of inquiry.

Myth alert!

"Signing the quality policy is a demonstration of the commitment to ISO by the leadership."

Myth busted!

Clearly, leadership is far more than putting a signature on some 'executive order.' We see world leaders do this regularly, yet totally fail at leading their respective countries through all manner of privation. The reasons are manifold.

Top tips

The leadership should be assigned roles as process owners, which involves the following:

- **Know the requirements** – including customer, regulatory/statutory (if applicable), and ISO 9001-related requirements
- **Know the process** – including the inputs, controls, resources (people's roles, responsibilities, etc.), and outputs
- **Know the performance** – including the goals/objectives of the process, what is measured and what is monitored, and the current results
- **Know the improvements** – including what needs corrective action and improving

Use the above as the basis of meeting the requirements of "Management Review" (9.3) and focus on the third and fourth items relating to the management review agenda, as applicable to the specific process – presented by the process owner. Reference can be made to the results of the internal audits as validation of the details (the 'story') behind the process owner's reporting.

The sub-clause of "Customer Focus" (5.1.2) is an interesting one, especially when viewed from a commercial perspective

– or to put it another way: "It's not quality at any cost." If the aim of any organization is to satisfy a customer's needs, then establishing those needs is predominantly the role of the sales and marketing functions. Prices and delivery are usually part of establishing needs and expectations, along with product/service specifications. Agreement usually comes in the form of a contract. The product or service is delivered and some attempt may be made to 'survey' the customer as to their level of satisfaction – with varying degrees of success or accuracy. But did the organization make any money? What was the cost of goods sold? The margin or mark-up? 25%? What is eroding that margin? The supplier rejects because the procurement/purchasing policy is to buy at lowest cost? The number of design engineering changes processed due to manufacturability/testability issues? The unrecorded costs of the processing associated with scrap, rework, and repaired product? Any warranty and recall costs? All these, and others, determine the actual revenue associated with doing business. Who is paying for that? To be truly customer focused, an organization needs to get these costs identified, accurately measured, under control, and improved – for survival.

Planning (6)

The first sub-clause of this section of the Standard is entitled "Actions to address risk and opportunities." (6.1)

This requirement is intended to direct the organization to take those issues identified in considering the context of the organization – the (prioritized) results of a SWOT analysis plus the understanding of the needs and expectations of those interested parties – and put them into a plan that includes integration of the actions into the processes.

As previously discussed, the prevailing 'silver tsunami' of retiring, skilled, and competent workers is likely to put an organization's ability to deliver good quality at risk. The organization should, therefore, plan to address this risk and identify what is to be done to mitigate the effects. Clearly, this is a risk that affects many organizations, so simply hiring replacement skilled workers isn't a viable option. What to do?

Once commonplace, apprenticeships were a way of developing the next generation of skilled workers, but those programs had slipped into obscurity. Simply put, most organizations employ workers who might have been apprentices, but the training processes have not been maintained. Add to this secondary schools and many community colleges have cut back on those educational programs that prepared younger people for work and the organization cannot sit on its hands hoping someone else will step in. Furthermore, many organizations' training processes typically only deal with the basics of onboarding and on-the-job training specific to the narrow focus of product/process tasks.

What's needed is for the organization to develop a process, within the QMS, that will create the skilled workforce it will need in the future. Fortunately, experience shows that, because many others are in a similar boat, further education colleges and schools also are developing and offering the supporting educational programs in the much-needed development of skills.

This section of the Standard also contains a couple of guidance notes regarding risk treatment, including options for addressing risks, such as avoidance, elimination of sources of risk, changing the likelihood or consequences, sharing the risk, or retaining the risk by informed decision or even pursuing an opportunity through taking a risk. Opportunities are detailed as something an organization may identify as 'new': a process, product, technology, et'. It's not clear that 'new' and 'risk' are often viewed as going hand in glove.

Quality Objectives (section 6.2) are required to be established at relevant functions, levels, and processes. This gives a great deal of latitude for the organization to think about the link to the quality policy (which itself is linked to the context of the organization) to establish the goals for the QMS. Before setting objectives, it is worth noting that they should be:

- Measurable
- Take into account applicable requirements
- Be relevant to product conformity and enhance customer satisfaction
- Be monitored
- Be communicated
- Be updated as appropriate

The quality objectives are also required to be maintained as documented information (but the Standard doesn't say where they are to be documented or how).

Myth alert!

"We'll set KPIs for all our processes and departments."

Myth busted!

Defining KPIs in and of themselves is not likely to be most effective. It's not unusual to have functions and departments select their own KPIs without consideration of the impacts on other areas of the organization or even the relevance of such KPIs.

By considering the basic tenets of quality management that relate to the era of total quality, and embrace the principles of product and process being done 'On Time' and 'In Specification', we get OTIS as a place to start flowing down objectives to the processes of the QMS. It is understood that in many cases, 100% is a nice idea but impractical – hence setting some level that is attainable and provides room for improvement:

On-time delivery of product as a goal might realistically become 95%.

First pass yield from a process might reasonably become 97%.

Having established these across the (core) processes, it follows that there may be an opportunity to set objectives at an individual level.

Top tip

When setting objectives, make them SMART. A (technical) member of staff might set the following:

- ***S = Specific:***

  "We want you to write technical blog articles to support our marketing on social media."

- ***M = Measurable:***

  "About 300 words for each article."

- ***A = Achievable:***

  "Do you think you can do that in the coming year?"

- ***R = Relevant:***

  "The articles should cover topics such as A, B, C, and D."

- ***T = Time based:***

  "We'd like one article every three months."

Be selective on which processes have OTIS applied to them. It is easy to overwhelm people with multiple objectives. It might be tempting to set objectives for the document or records control processes, but these are hardly likely to directly affect the achievement of customer satisfaction.

The last requirement in Planning is devoted to planning of changes to the QMS, when the organization determines they are needed. There is a reference back to 4.4 and that changes need to be carried out in a planned manner. These should be viewed as changes identified at a strategic level, not the day-to-day changes that are covered within other clauses of the Standard, such as changes to customers' requirements, product designs, and process controls.

It is well established that changes can be the source of problems without a robust plan. The requirements list the considerations the organization should make in its planning:

- The purpose of the change and consequences

- The integrity of the QMS
- The availability of resources
- The allocation or reallocation of responsibilities and authorities

Support (7)

This requirement of the Standard deals with those parts of the QMS that support or are in place to enable the other processes to function more effectively. It includes:

Resources (7.1.1)

An organization must be selective at what it takes on, in the name of satisfying customers' needs and expectations. People can move heaven and earth, but you have to give them time, tools, and a budget as a minimum. The resources are necessary for the whole of the QMS implementation and for process operation and control. These include the following:

People (7.1.2)

Despite the saying, *"The factory of the future will be run by a man and a dog. The man is there to feed the dog and the dog is there to keep the man away from the machinery,"* most organizations need people to do work to satisfy their customers' demands and for the effective operation of the QMS. Oddly, having mentioned People, there is no reference to the other sub-clauses (7.1.6, 7.2, 7.3, 7.4) that go on to develop more on the theme of People…

Infrastructure (7.1.3)

Try as we might, it is a practical impossibility to produce a good-quality product, even with all the necessary people, without the appropriate equipment, power, computers, information, and so on. The infrastructure requirements to ensure product conformity should be identified and provided by the organization, including such items as process equipment, buildings, utilities, workspace, and services.

Environment for the Operation of Processes (7.1.4)

In step with the above, the work environment can also have an effect on product conformity. There is a note underneath the ISO 9001 requirement that defines typical environmental factors, such as noise, humidity, lighting, or weather. Others might include temperature, air quality, dust, etc. These factors must be managed.

Monitoring & Measuring Resources (7.1.5)

This requirement of ISO 9001 is possibly one of the most confused and abused, being open to interpretation, especially by those with minimal understanding of the topic. Commonly called 'calibration' and applied to equipment used to measure product characteristics and/or process parameters, the section starts by simply stating that measuring resources are provided to ensure valid and reliable results. It goes on to state that the resources provided are suitable for the measuring and monitoring activities and are maintained to ensure fitness for purpose. It doesn't even mention calibration or verification! Interesting, isn't it?

A sub-section called "Measurement traceability" points out that it may be a requirement (Customer? Regulatory?) or if the organization considers it essential to provide confidence in the validity of measuring, results can be calibrated, verified, or both.

Myth alert!

"All measuring equipment has to have a 'calibration' sticker on it to show the date calibrated, recall date, etc."

Myth busted!

The problem with stickers is they do not stick, especially in some work environments. It is usual to have an identification number or similar on the device and use that to trace the record of calibration/verification.

Myth alert!

"Calibration must occur annually."

Myth busted!

Calibration is really a function of use, for most common forms of gauges. Selecting and then sticking to a time-based calibration frequency can cause big (cost) issues that come from not calibrating frequently enough or too frequently. Use the data from periodic verifications to determine the calibration frequency.

Myth alert!

"All measuring equipment must be calibrated."

Myth busted!

There are three classes of measuring equipment:

1. Calibration/verification not required (for example, an engineer's six-inch steel rule)
2. Verification before use (for example, a machine operator's micrometer)

3. Calibration (for example, the equipment used to 'master' verification or perform measurements where confidence in results is paramount)

Myth alert!

"Calibration includes adjustment to correct the reading."

Myth busted!

The act of calibration simply provides details of how the measuring equipment is performing compared to a known standard. If it is found to be performing out of specification/tolerance, then it may be a) still usable and b) incapable of being adjusted or c) replaced.

Myth alert!

"Uncalibrated equipment should be labeled 'for reference only'."

Myth busted!

Using such a label is not control! It is abdicating control. People need to know, if they use measuring equipment, whether they can have confidence in the results – especially if it helps them to determine the quality of the product they are processing.

Myth alert!

"Only equipment used for final inspection needs calibration."

Myth busted!

Depending upon the cost/value of the product to the organization, added to it through processing, it might be disastrous to discover that decisions made earlier about items tested and inspected may be out of specification at a final check. Relying only on final checks using calibrated devices can be expensive compared to intermediate checks with – as a minimum – verified devices.

Myth alert!

"Calibration is expensive."

Myth busted!

Yes, indeed, it can be. However, not knowing the condition of the devices used for measuring and testing – especially if they are used to avoid rejection of product by customers or to suppliers – can cost a lot more.

Top tips

Don't overcomplicate the control of measuring equipment by calibrating everything – it is wasteful and unnecessary.

In practical terms, the organization should simply consider this question: "If we make a measurement and can argue about the results (possibly rejections and associated unplanned costs) affecting customers, a regulatory body, or a supplier, then having our equipment calibrated is a good option – to ensure traceability to a known 'master' that is used nationally or even internationally. Internally, equipment may be verified using a known 'master' device to confirm it is working correctly. A simple record should be maintained, too.

The terms 'calibration' and 'verification' are often used interchangeably when describing how measuring equipment is controlled and maintained as fit for use. Calibration is the science of understanding how far from a true value the result from measuring a characteristic (product, process, etc.) is likely to be. The true value is correctly known as the 'measurand' and the process of measurement of a characteristic will be influenced in some manner by factors affecting the measuring results.

The calibration results of the device(s) used when measuring do affect the result and should be known before deciding if the characteristic meets the specification.

It is tempting to simply contract with a supplier of calibration services, such as a laboratory that is accredited to ISO/IEC 17025, and place a purchase order stating "calibrate to manufacturers' specifications," but this may not be sufficient. Carefully review the services offered – most labs provide a menu of services – to determine the one that is most (cost) effective.

Organizational Knowledge (7.1.6)

How does an organization know what it knows about how to satisfy customers' needs and expectations for products and services? Clearly, it isn't about specific technologies, processes, equipment, people, suppliers, etc. It must be a combination of all these and more. Reference to the notes at the foot of the page shows that ISO recognizes it is experience and based on sources that are both internal and external.

The Standard is pretty clear: Maintain the knowledge (it doesn't say it needs to be in any form of documentation) and make it available.

Top tips

Many organizations have ways to capture what is learned during production of products. Operators make marginal notes on job cards/shop travelers or other documentation that accompanies the materials around the processes, as it is transformed. Similarly, if we consider those organizations that depend heavily upon the skills of their workforce, having some kind of mentoring program (see also section 6 comments) would be a way to ensure continuity of knowledge and also consider some form of succession planning.

With the advent of 'Industry 4.0' (or Fourth Industrial Revolution), which depends on nine interlacing technologies, clearly no organization is going to possess the relevant knowledge of these in the early days of adoption. It is likely, therefore, that external sources will need to be engaged, including manufacturers and suppliers of technology equipment, places of higher education, and government-sponsored entities, if the endeavor is to be successful.

Whatever course of action is taken, the intent is to minimize the risk of reinventing the wheel or doing the same thing and expecting a different result, which can befall such implementations.

There aren't too many myths associated with this requirement, other than perhaps to attempt to document everything that isn't likely to be a) simple or b) effective.

Use the QMS to manage any improvement opportunities, through management review and the change control requirements, and the next section of ISO 9001.

Competence (7.2)

With a strong link to the Operation requirements (section 8), specifically 8.3 and 8.5, the need for competent personnel is much more than simply training people. Training makes people dangerous!

Myth alert!

"Everyone needs training on ISO."

Myth busted!

Few people need training – or indeed competency – in the ISO 9001 requirements. What's most important is to understand the roles, responsibilities, and authorities of a job, know the process required, and know what to do in the event that everything doesn't go to plan – how to deal with the process and any results that do not conform.

Myth alert!

"We 'grandfathered' people into their jobs."

Myth busted!

Things change and our grandparents didn't keep up!

Myth alert!

"We have training certificates for everyone."

Myth busted!

Training is just one of the options to help people become competent. A certificate doesn't mean the person can apply what they learned, and some training just isn't effective – so the certificate is meaningless.

Myth alert!

"We have new starters sign off with their supervisor that they understand their job."

Myth busted!

It's not a bad place to start, but without defining what the required competencies are and then demonstrating them, what's the point of the signatures?

Competency is defined in the vocabulary document ISO 9000 as:

"ability to apply knowledge and skills to achieve intended results." (3.10.4)

Why can't the grandfathering card be played? After all, some people have been working at their jobs a long time.

Answer: There is a need to determine and demonstrate competency for personnel who perform work that affects quality. Although there are many theories surrounding how adults become competent, there are generally accepted phases[1] that describe the progression:

1. Unconscious incompetence
2. Conscious incompetence
3. Conscious competence
4. Unconscious competence

It would be easy to assume that an experienced person is someone who has reached unconscious competence, and could be grandfathered into their job. That would be potentially a missed opportunity, partly because these are not concrete phases.

An article in a British motorcycle enthusiasts' magazine discussed the background to why significant numbers of British motorcyclists were being killed in crashes on the roads. There were some shocking statistics, including that no one else was involved, just the bike and its rider. Another was the average age of the victims, which was 50 years. These were very experienced bikers, with many years of motorcycling informing their riding skills in addition to any tests they may have taken to receive a license.

What was causing these riders to get into these lethal situations? Analyzing the facts associated with each crash revealed that changes had occurred, which had affected the riders' abilities, such as eyesight acuity, speed of reactions, and the power and capabilities of the motorcycles being ridden. All have an effect on the riders' competencies, compared to their early years of riding. The final analysis of

---

[1] Martin Broadwell c. February 1969.

these events showed that just because someone attains phase 4 – unconscious competency – doesn't mean they stay there!

Top tips

Awareness (7.3)

It might be obvious to many, but awareness isn't the same as training or education. In today's industrial environments, it is common practice to employ people to do specific tasks or activities that are part of a much more complex and complicated process. The scale of the production processes – take, for example, the UK's Cross rail construction project, or building a car or ship. Large numbers of people with a narrow focus on specific work activities, which are all interlinked and can have significant impact on each other. Being aware of (quality) policies, the (quality) objectives, how their work affects the overall performance (quality) of the product, and the implications of not conforming to the QMS requirements are intended to provide greater ownership by individuals.

Communications (7.4)

Although it may be seemingly important that the organization communicates that it is using ISO 9001 to develop a formalized approach to its process controls, too much reference to ISO can be counterproductive.

In an effective implementation, most of the emphasis goes on ensuring people are aware of the fundamentals of the organization's QMS, and why these are important to them in getting their work done, for regulatory compliance, to ensure customers' needs are met, etc.

As with an organization that sets SMART objectives for its people, the communication of progress toward meeting those objectives, the 'wins,' the 'losses,' are all important to be known throughout.

Management should not treat performance like a game of Texas Hold 'Em poker. Everyone has a stake in the results, after all.

There are many ways that communication may take place of the reasons for an organization to use ISO 9001, including why the organization has chosen to formally define and implement a QMS, and ultimately become certified by a third party. This isn't really "training" and 99% of personnel don't need to know much of the "back story". Far better to describe these through the use of 'brown bag' lunch meetings, newsletters, staff meetings, and other events – and no records are required!

Top tips

Communication is a two-way street. Tell people what is going on. Success breeds success. People rally to make improvements when given half a chance. Allow them to tell management what is important to them to know. Have them contribute gains, best practices, etc. Reward participation in events such as problem solving (using the

'8D' – 8 Disciplines – method. It is the eighth 'D': Reward the team).

Documented Information (7.5)

The requirement for the organization to include documented information as part of its approach to developing a QMS is in two distinct parts:

1. That documented information which is required by ISO 9001:2015, including:
   - The scope of the QMS
   - Quality objectives
   - Quality policy
2. That documented information which is required by the organization to be included within its QMS.

This is to support the operation of the processes of the QMS. Once again, the Standard does not make it clear that there are other clauses that should be considered when attempting to determine what is required, in practical terms, to be documented. If we consider the Introduction, there are several reasons listed that provide background on which to base the consideration for creating and maintaining documentation.

Furthermore, if the "Needs and expectations of interested parties" are also understood, it should be seen that documentation may be required by customers, regulatory agencies (if applicable), and the personnel of the organization – to help them achieve objectives, as a training aid for people new to a job, to ensure control or processes, and to maintain knowledge of how work is accomplished. A lot of (good) reasons!

Myth alert!

"We will structure our documentation like this diagram:"

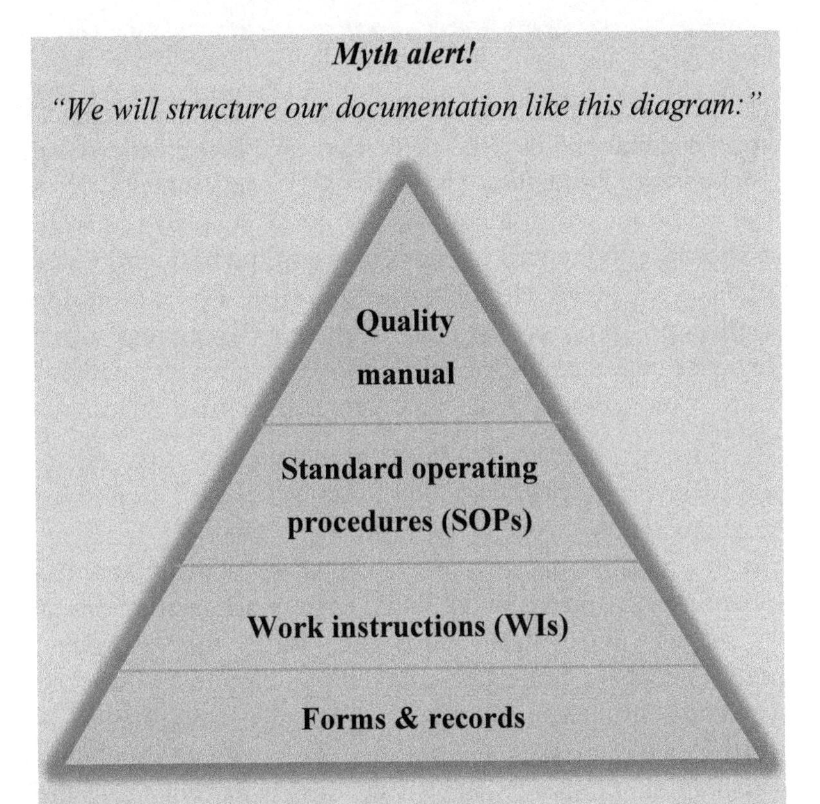

Figure 2: Documentation structure

Myth busted!

In previous version of ISO 9001, it was only ever implied that a QMS had layers or levels of documentation. The 2015 edition allows an organization to create whatever documentation it sees fit and simply control it.

Myth alert!

"You should document your process so that if no one turns up for work, anyone can do the job."

Myth busted!

If, as the Standard suggests, we apply risk-based thinking to such a situation, it is unlikely that any organization will encounter this situation. The COVID-19 pandemic may have put a severe strain on the availability of people to a) work and b) be experienced in one or more of the basic processes of an organization. Hence, the need to write a sales or design engineering process down for inexperienced people is such a low risk as to be ignored. Write processes for your methods of operation, considering competent people are doing them.

Previous versions of ISO 9001, especially the very earliest editions from 1987 – 2000, referred to a variety of documentation types, specifically quality manuals, documented procedures, and, in relation to manufacturing processes, the provision of documented work instructions as a means to control processes. With the additional requirements to generate records, it was easy to see how the pyramid structure became the default interpretation – justified by an explanation that the standard operating procedures represented the 'what' had to be done and the work instructions represented the 'how.' This oversimplification of the requirements and need for documentation as a key component of the organization's QMS became one of the biggest and long-lasting myths. It also served to drive away many smaller organizations that often saw the whole thing as a mountain of documents of dubious benefit.

Top tips

The design of documentation can achieve a lot of features without creating a bureaucracy. The 'smart design' of documents for processes can include both instructions and a record that the process was completed – within the same document. Consider the place of technology. While paperwork may be cumbersome, technology solutions such as tablets, smartphones, and HDMI smart TVs bring their own challenges including opening up the organization to the risks of cybersecurity breaches and the associated costs.

Putting your drawings, specification, instructions, process descriptions, ERP, CRM, and countless data records in the Cloud can be fraught with complications if there is no one on the team who understands. ISO 9001 references "documented information" some 38 times. Consider how that documented information should also become "secured, documented information" and it can be seen that it is an extensive task. Much, if not all, of that documentation can be classified by the following:

- **C** – confidentiality
- **I** – integrity
- **A** – availability

These are the CIA triad of information security – a topic that we read about daily as adversely affecting large organizations. What is not always reported is the significant number of small/medium-sized organizations that also fall foul of cyber attacks – even those perpetrated by teenagers who did nothing but wipe all the calibration data off a hard drive.

Operation (8)

Operational Planning and Control (8.1)

In section 6 we reviewed the strategic planning required of the organization. In this requirement, the focus is on the planning at a tactical level.

Myth alert!

"Our processes are simple, we don't need to plan."

"We don't have time to plan our processes."

Myth busted!

It is the organization's responsibility to determine the processes needed for the QMS and their sequence and interaction. In smaller organizations, this almost becomes the plan for the way that customer inputs are turned into deliverable products. Other organizations – often those that perform multiple, often more complex operations – use a 'shop traveler' or 'operations sheet' or similar, which defines each step or operation, in sequence, transforming the raw material into a completed product. It is also common for the quality control checks required to verify the product is correct to specification to be included on the plan.

More complex products, or where required by a contractual arrangement with a customer, sometimes dictate a more detailed document, which may be called a quality plan.

Requirements for Products and Services (8.2)

Myth alert!

"We call this 'contract review'."

"Our customer only gave us verbal instructions, there is no contract."

"This is just about having a process for customer orders."

Myth busted!

Quality, in all respects, begins with determining what the product being offered (for sale) is and what the customer wants, with the intent of coming to some form of agreement to supply! These requirements fit the convention of quoting, order processing, and change orders, in whatever form these take.

Customer Communication (8.2.1)

To avoid misunderstandings, and hence create opportunities for customer dissatisfaction, there must be control over communications, whether that's regarding the organization's website and claims for products, performance, availability, and so on. Similarly, how customer inquiries, quotes, ordering, and changes to these are handled must, as with any process, be controlled, avoiding errors.

Handling feedback to elicit the most accurate and useful information takes a special relationship and understanding – and is probably best handled by a few individuals. Of course, once the feedback is obtained, it is likely that the organization's customers will expect to see the results of some action.

Although not prescribed by ISO 9001, providing plan B to take care of customers in the event that plan A didn't work out is key to maintaining good, if not perfect, customer relationships.

Determination of Requirements for Products and Services (8.2.2)

The requirement touches on four basic factors:

1. Determining customer requirements
2. Determining requirements not stated by the customer but still necessary for use, where known
3. Statutory and regulatory requirements
4. Anything else thought necessary by the organization

Often, with innovative product designs, these factors are determined during development through market/customer research, some time before sales or agreement to supply the customer occurs. Indeed, a note indicates that the review may be of product catalogs or advertising materials.

Review of Requirements Related to the Product (8.2.2)

Before any commitment is made to supply customers, a review must be undertaken. Once again, the review isn't simply a case of checking a customer order for the stated requirements – although that is important – but on receipt of a customer request for quote (RFQ/RFP), on receipt of an order, and when change orders are received by the organization.

The purpose of the review is to ensure that:

1. The product requirements are defined

2. The order and any previous offer (proposal, for example) are compared and differences resolved
3. The organization has the ability to meet the stated requirements
4. Records of the reviews and actions that arise are maintained

There are situations where organizations that take orders from customers verbally (telesales), and without any documents being used, cannot reasonably perform a review. In such cases, confirmation of the customer's requirements is necessary. This can take the form of an order confirmation (email, fax, etc.) or by verbally confirming with the customer (which often is recorded). Design & Development of products and services (8.3)

Product design and development is where a lot of problems in manufacturing, with suppliers, and in the marketplace can be avoided with an effective process and relevant controls, responsibilities, authorities, etc.

Myth alert!

"The product design and development process cannot be measured."

Myth busted!

The three key measurements of the NPD process are:

Quality, time, and cost

Myth alert!

"Design engineers need the freedom to be creative."

Myth busted!

While it is true that creativity and innovation are to be encouraged, these should still meet the three key measurements and also ensure that design for manufacturability, design for testability, etc. criteria are still met.

Myth alert!

"Following ISO will slow down the process."

Myth busted!

The time spent in a well-developed new product more than makes up for the time/cost and aggravation associated with the inevitable post-release changes, warranty and customer dissatisfaction.

Time to market often is a huge part of driving new product developments and their introduction. The needs to wow the market, beat competitors, etc. are powerful factors. No one wants an underdeveloped product that, once released, takes unplanned resources (time/money) to resolve manufacturability issues, warranty costs, and potentially loss of market share through unsatisfied customer experiences – all of which should be added to the original development schedules/budgets for a true picture.

The product design and development process requirements of ISO 9001 are fairly simple and intended to ensure that the organization only designs products that can be produced, installed, and serviced without problems and that are safe for use – and customers get what they really want!

Often known as the new product development cycle (NPD or similar), the ISO 9001 requirements form a basic framework for controls that should enable not reduce creativity. The ISO 9001 8.3 requirements cover:

- Design Development Planning
- Design and Development Inputs
- Design and Development Outputs
- Design and Development Reviews
- Design and Development Verification
- Design and Development Validation
- Control of Design and Development Changes

Experience shows that there are a few key indications of how effective the design and development process is, and they are easily identified and measured:

- The number of post-release design changes (not resulting from customer inputs)
- The 'on time' and 'on budget' performance
- The retention of engineering staff

The last point is directly linked to the first; however, it is rarely seen in this light. Similarly, where parts of the new product under development include aspects that must be obtained from suppliers – particularly those working to specifications developed by the organization – early supplier selection is critical as it is proven that their input to the design is invaluable. Not only are changes avoided but also the high costs of supply disruptions from rejections, etc.

Let's take a look at a typical new product design engineering process to understand the indicators of an ineffective process:

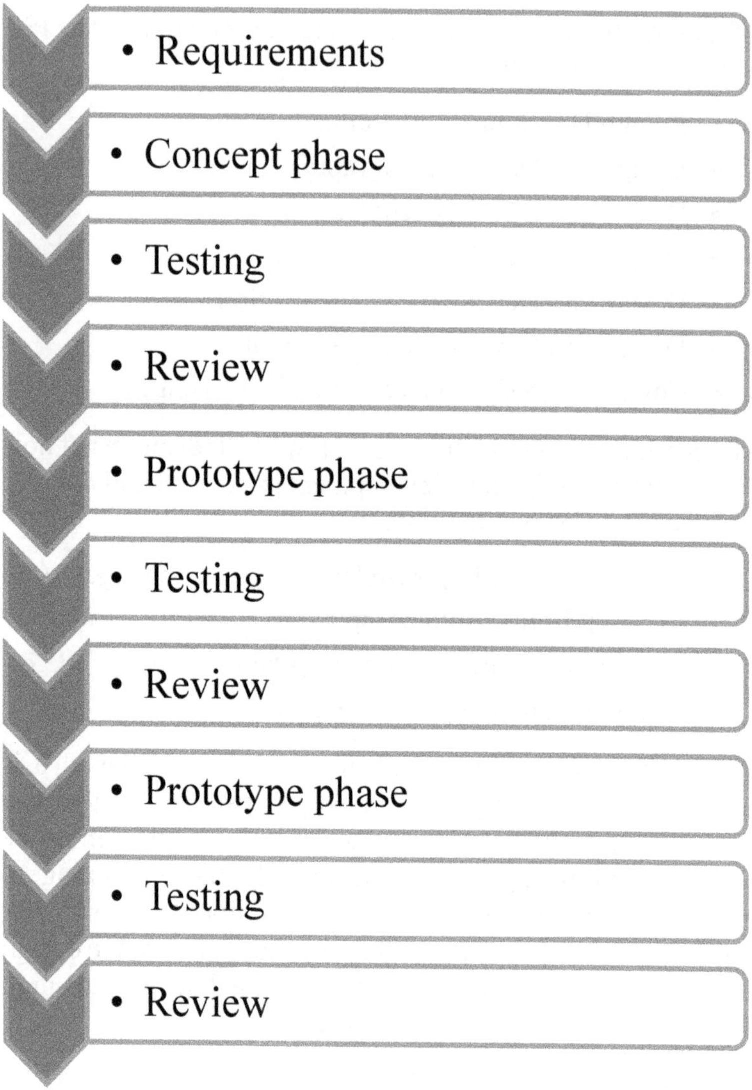

- Requirements
- Concept phase
- Testing
- Review
- Prototype phase
- Testing
- Review
- Prototype phase
- Testing
- Review

Figure 3: New product design engineering process

A robust product design and development process should release a set of product specifications to manufacturing and (as applicable) servicing organizations (whether those activities are performed internally by the organization or by its suppliers) that can be produced within the capabilities of those manufacturing and service processes. The product of the design engineering process is not unlike the product of the manufacturing process(es) in that it should not be necessary to 'touch it twice' to make it correctly (to specification) and it must be delivered on time and at the planned cost. Therefore, three key indicators of the effectiveness of the new product design and development process are:

1. Delivery to schedule
2. Development cost on budget
3. Post-release changes

This last point has been well studied because the cost of changing a product design, after release to production, is a significant factor. It is suggested that a fault found in the design phases might cost X to rectify, would cost ten times that value (10X) if detected in production, and 100 times more (100X) if found while in customers' hands.

Often, it is necessary to process product design changes once the product has been released to be produced, either by the organization's own manufacturing function or by its suppliers. Often, such changes are given to those design engineers who have recently qualified and been recruited, much to their chagrin.

Newly qualified product design engineers are probably under the impression that once they take a position in industry, designing new products is exciting and they will get to use their expertise, bringing innovative and creative ideas to light. In reality, they may be assigned (initially) to work on existing product design changes. This presents two challenges for these engineers:

1. It is often very difficult to re-engineer a product
2. They are often not sufficiently experienced to re-engineer products and this can be demotivating

A study of major Japanese new product introductions showed that the majority of changes to product designs occurred before release into the marketplace, and that few changes were undertaken after that. The results? Improved customer perception, lower warranty costs, happier service staff, and improved market image, to name a few.

Control of Externally Provided Processes, Products and Services (8.4)

Myth alert!

"An approved supplier list is required."

Myth busted!

Most of us who are responsible for buying food, cars, services, and the things to make our lives tolerable have a way to evaluate suppliers of those things. We use criteria such as cost, product availability, service level, location, and so on. We rarely create even a mental list. ISO 9001 expects a similar, if more formal, process – and records of those evaluations against the criteria. But certainly no list, per se. For some organizations, a list of preferred suppliers might be useful, of course.

Myth alert!

"Suppliers need to be audited."

Myth busted!

For certain types of suppliers, an organization may wish to perform pre-award audits or even audits of any corrective actions undertaken after experiencing deliveries of a non-conforming product. However, ISO 9001 certainly doesn't require such audits.

Myth alert!

"All suppliers should be ISO certified."

Myth busted!

'Let the buyer beware' continues to apply in the supply chain regarding the use of suppliers with ISO certification. Care should be taken to ensure that the certificate is a) current, b) has a scope that covers the product/services being procured, and c) was issued by a certification body that is accredited by an IAF-member accreditation body. Details can be found at *www.iaf.nu*.

Care should still be exercised by the organization when considering suppliers with an ISO 9001 certificate, since it is not unknown for certificates to be issued that a) have inaccurate scopes (often including 'design' when no such work is undertaken) and b) the QMS isn't compliant with the current version of ISO 9001! Bizarre but true in a small number of cases.

Top tip

When selecting key suppliers, care should always be taken to assure that any certification is accurate and that the supplier organization is implementing a QMS that delivers product quality, as planned. An annual audit by a third party is too infrequent to detect changes in performance that can seriously affect the organization's confidence in the supply chain. Certainly, process controls should be in place at even a basic level, which should prevent the added costs of the purchasers expending resources on supplier development.

Production and Service Provision (8.5)

Control of Production and Service Provision (8.5.1)

For an organization to produce a quality product (or service), it is generally held that the product-related processes must be carried out such that they are controlled. Although the requirements are seemingly simple, what is often missed is the concept behind controlling the production and service processes, which is to have 'standard work.' That is, each activity can be replicated over and over again, without variation, which may lead to a non-conforming product or process. A well-known example is a famous fast food restaurant chain, which has produced the same basic hamburger, serving billions by following the same process and methods, in every location, by thousands of people. Process control comes from one or more of the following:

- *"Availability of documented information defining:*

   - *Product characteristics, services provided, or activities*
   - *Results to be achieved*
   - *The availability and use of measuring and monitoring resources*
- *Implementing measuring and monitoring activities at appropriate stages to verify that process control or output criteria are met and acceptance criteria for products and services have also been met*
- *Use of suitable infrastructure and environment for process operation*
- *Appointment of competent personnel*
- *Validation and periodic revalidation of the ability to achieve planned results or the processes, where the results cannot be verified by subsequent measurement and monitoring*
- *Implementation of actions to prevent human error"*[2] (also known as mistake proofing and poka-yoke)

It is important to note that any one requirement should not be considered without reference to at least one other. This requirement of ISO 9001 specifically requires consideration of a significant number of others. Take the requirement for the "availability of documented information," for example. The addition of the words "as applicable" might be considered 'weasel words' as they allow us to weasel out of having to comply! So, is it justifiable to not make some kind

[2] ISO 9001:2015. For more information, visit: www.iso.org/standard/62085.html.

of documentation available to people performing product-related activities? A clue is in understanding the relationship to other ISO 9001 requirements that have influence on 8.5:

As noted previously, the people who are responsible for the control of a process may be assigned based upon competence (7.2). This may obviate the need for a document. However, we must not overlook the requirements from much earlier – the needs and expectations of interested parties. Surely there may be situations where:

- Customers will require some form of documentation to be used in production of what they are going to receive
- Regulatory agencies may require the organization to define documentation for control of processes
- Employees may benefit from having the process controls being documented to ensure effective training, for reference, for consistency, etc.

Furthermore, the use of documentation regarding production processes is a way of maintaining the contemporary knowledge of how the process is being operated – often called best practice.

Myth alert!

"All processes need work instructions."

Myth busted!

Some form of work instruction is an option for controlling processes, but by no means a specific requirement. Customers may make it a requirement to gain confidence in the way their product is made. The organization also may decide – for many reasons including knowledge preservation, training, etc. – but work instructions are just one means of process control. A balance may need to be struck with the competency of the persons performing the work.

Myth alert!

"We test the first and last part to tell us if the others meet the specification."

Myth busted!

Typically, where there is some (significant) volume of products being provided, the validity of taking a 'first off' and 'last off' is not an effective way to ensure all other products are to specification. Despite the Standard not clearly addressing the topic, if a process is to be operated and "in control", concepts such as the causes of variation (common and special) must be understood and used to inform a suitable plan of inspections and tests.

Myth alert!

"Once we set the process up, as long as we are checking a few in production, we are good! There's not much variation."

Myth busted!

As with the previous myth, it is well established that even in control, processes vary over time and that this inexorable 'drift' needs to be studied. Knowing the three phases of installation quality, operational quality, and performance quality (IQ, OQ, PQ) is important in avoiding unforeseen quality issues and the attendant increased costs.

For some processes, the quality of the resulting output cannot be reasonably (economically or practically) tested or inspected. This requirement of ISO 9001 defines what the organization must do to ensure that an acceptable product is produced. For many, determining what processes fall into this category can be a challenge. In previous versions of ISO 9001, these processes were known as "special processes," but even this didn't adequately describe them – for such processes are quite common for organizations that perform them and not, therefore, considered special!

Which processes fall into the category of needing validation/revalidation? Some typical examples include:

- Gluing and bonding
- Welding, brazing and soldering
- Heat treatment and sterilization
- Plating, painting, and coating
- Torquing screw fasteners

As anyone who has attempted to repair a broken item at home (let's say a vase) knows, following the instructions on the glue packaging is of vital importance to a good result. We are told to clean the mating parts, often with some proprietary degreaser/spirits/cleaner. The mating surfaces being joined might be roughened with sandpaper to provide a key for the adhesive. Of course, the temperature may also need to be between some values that represent a typical summer's day.

Having prepared the surfaces, it may be necessary to coat the mating parts with the adhesive and allow it to cure (at least partially, when it is less tacky and dry to the touch). At this point, the mating parts may be required to be brought together and held, often under some pressure for a defined time. We also know it is tempting to test our newly created join in the precious vase to see if it is fixed! We might try to break the joint! How quickly our surprise turns to frustration when the joint does break and we have to start over! Oh, the temptation to check the joint once more…

Performing a test or similar on a sample from the process is a way to reduce the risk of failure in the other products being processed. This is still fraught with potential problems and can be wasteful too. We are left with imponderable questions about how representative the sample is. How is that validated? By the time steps have been taken to check that, the requirements for process validation have been met, so there is now no point in sacrificing a sample!

It is also worth considering that processes are subject to variation. Despite the fact that the ISO requirements do not mention it, for most organizations that produce any appreciable volume of products, their processes – particularly equipment – are subject to an amount of variation that can take the product out of specification.

Top tips

The idea of a quality (product) result that comes from gaining control over the inputs, resources, process parameters, and measurements, such that the output will be as planned and meets specification, isn't an alien concept. Fast food providers do it daily – some really famous restaurants have been doing this millions and millions of times. No inspection after the fact! No one would buy a 1/4lb burger with teeth marks in it and a chunk missing.

The organization should strive to emphasize the control over processing to minimize the amount and type of 'after the fact' inspection because it is often too late in the process and, hence, the associated costs are higher than the already high cost of inspection. This previous list of examples are the usual suspects for this type of process control treatment, when – in all seriousness – all processes should be planned to be treated this way.

Identification and Traceability (8.5.2)

Myth alert!

"It is obvious what the product is from looking at it."

Myth busted!

While it might be clear to most what type of product is being processed in terms of size, shape, weight, or other unique characteristic, identification also includes its status of activities like inspection and testing.

Myth alert!

"Our products have to be traceable to the raw materials."

Myth busted!

This is a requirement of ISO 9001 that employs the 'weasel words' of 'when it is necessary!' This leaves the organization some latitude to decide when it deems necessary. It should be clear that – especially when products look similar – some form of identification may be necessary to prevent problems caused by mixing them. The methods used for identification can be diverse: identification on the part, location, container labeling are common options. It is not required when there is sufficient difference that there is no confusion about which product is which and people do not have to keep asking supervision!

The second requirement – the status of the product with regard to measuring and monitoring – is clearer. The organization "shall." The reason? An untested/uninspected product should not be allowed to progress and only a known 'good' product should make it to the point of being shipped to a customer! Also consider that retesting/inspecting a product – when no one can tell if it has/has not been checked – is expensive, causes delays, and is not value-added. Everyone knows how frustrating it can be when you change batteries and get the old and new ones mixed up! Segregate, tag, or mark them in some way to ensure they don't get mixed.

Traceability is one of those where, again, 'weasel words' are used. Simply put, traceability allows the organization to limit its exposure to the risk of quality problems as far up and down the supply chain as is practical or necessary. Often driven by regulatory requirements, unique identification is normally applied to a product and/or its associated packaging.

Property Belonging to Customers or External Providers (8.5.3)

Customer property is anything the customer gives the organization that is used in the deliverables to that customer. Items falling into this category tend to include raw materials (often bought in bulk to save money) and products intended for repair/service.

When dealing with customer property, it is normal to invoke a number of other requirements of ISO 9001 to handle the processes that deliver the property to the customer.

A traditional application of this would be a car taken into a dealership or garage for servicing or repairs. The car represents customer property and, as such, it is the dealership's responsibility to:

- Take care of it to ensure no damage is done to the car while it is in their custody, by them or while parked on their premises (e.g. vandalized).
- Report anything found during the work that may affect the ability of the work to be carried out. For example, if the car had a non-functioning parking brake, the dealership would probably not want to be responsible, since the car may run away down a slope when 'parked.'

Organizations that service and/or repair products as part of the quality management scope (see section 4) – perhaps in addition to designing and manufacturing them – deal with customers' property as a core process. It is not unusual for a product to appear on the receiving dock with minimal/zero instruction on what the customer requires to be done or even a purchase order. In such a case, it is up to the organization to determine what work is required and report this to the customer, as the basis for establishing agreement on cost and return/delivery.

Myth alert!

"We need a whole set of procedures to meet this requirement."

If we consider the requirements and compare them to others, we can see that many other processes or the QMS are set up to handle similar situations, but with another focus or scope:

- Operational planning and control (8.1)
- Requirements for products (8.2)
- Control of externally provided products (8.4)
- Production control (8.5)
- Release (8.6)
- Control of non-conforming outputs (8.7)
- And so on…

Myth busted!

Employ the processes that exist to deal with receiving products, processing them, making sure people who do work are competent, inspection and testing, quoting the work to be done, non-conformance control, labeling and packaging/shipping, except ensure they cover the handling of products owned by the organization's customers.

Preservation (8.5.4)

Happily, there do not appear to be many common myths with this requirement. It is generally understood that it is important to take care of everything, from incoming raw materials, through work in progress, to final product. Preservation can apply not only to the product, keeping it to specification and free of damage caused by neglect, physical damage, etc., but also preservation of quantity.

Keeping an accurate inventory – by quantity and location (where it is applicable to the product) – is key in ensuring customer requirements can be met, and production isn't halted awaiting the correct quantity of materials and products.

Moving to post-delivery activities, 8.5.5, if the organization includes (within its QMS scope) activities beyond delivery, such as installation, commissioning, servicing, repair, decommissioning, and so on, there are considerations to be made:

- Statutory and regulatory requirements
- Potential undesired consequences associated with the products
- The nature, use, and intended lifetime of products
- Customer requirements and feedback

Although ISO 9001 is focused on product and service quality, here are some considerations that get remarkably close to environmental, health, and safety considerations. Experience shows that if customers' satisfaction is uppermost in an organization's consciousness, consideration must be given to conditions that affect the product's use and ultimately its disposal. For example, some vehicles sold in the US were designed and built with an electrical switch containing mercury. At the end of their useful life, the vehicles present a health and safety issue to the recycling businesses handling them as scrap. This situation could have been avoided during the new product design process. The electronics industry has a huge problem with personal computers being discarded. They feed the electronics counterfeiting industry with 'recycled' computer devices, and cyber crime with data from old hard drives.

Control of Changes (8.5.6)

As mentioned previously, *"The factory of the future will be run by a man and a dog. The man is there to feed the dog, the dog is there to keep the man away from the machinery"* is a quote attributed to Warren G Bennis. The message here is clear: Once a process is established as capable of meeting the necessary requirements and in control, don't let anyone fiddle with it! This is a concept that is common practice in the pharmaceutical and drug industries, due to oversight regulations. These exist because variation of process and product can have disastrous consequences and the product cannot be tested after the fact. ISO 9001 had already made it a requirement to change control documents, customers' orders, and product designs, so it is interesting to note that process change control has only been included since 2015!

If we draw a page from the automotive manufacturing world, in which changes are anathema, we will be able to see that the customer has to be notified or even approve changes in:

- Materials
- Production tooling
- People (shift working)
- Production machinery/methods
- Suppliers

Control of Non-conforming Outputs (8.7)

One of the reasons for monitoring and measuring a product is to detect any nonconformities (rejects) before they escape the organization and get to the customer. In regulated industries, this is especially important to ensure that defective products cannot be shipped and, therefore, used. When taking the basic controls into consideration, there are many myths that surround the controls for a non-conforming product.

Myth alert!

"Non-conforming products must be moved out of the production process, segregated, and/or locked away."

"Everything found non-conforming is 'scrap.' There is no need to record it, we can recycle it."

"It costs more to tag, record, and mess with the rejections than the value of the parts. We just toss them away."

"You need to have a material review board to decide what to do with a non-conforming product."

"We can allow the people who find the defects to decide what to do with the non-conforming product."

"All (product) nonconformities need a corrective action."

Myth busted!

When dealing with non-conformance, there are basic tenets that apply:

- Record it
- Identify it
- Control it to ensure it cannot find its way through the process and, hence, to the customer
- Have the right people decide what to do with it (it is worth money, after all)
- Monitor it and try to learn from the experience so that it is not repeated!

The full requirement for controls for a non-conforming product is often overlooked. The simple(r) aspects such as tagging or disposition are frequently given more emphasis than those that help to identify what caused the nonconformity and how it can be effectively processed subsequently. In particular, the decision on the disposition of a non-conforming product has to be given to the relevant authority and potentially by the customer.

There is certainly no specified need to treat each and every situation of nonconformity with a corrective action. Indeed, nothing else will bring the organization's QMS to a grinding halt quicker. Practically speaking, we know there is a likelihood of nonconformity when processing. In understanding process control, there are two causes of variation:

1. Common cause
2. Special cause

Common cause variation can be controlled and the risks of nonconformity mitigated. Special cause variation is just that: special. Things break. Without warning. They cause variation and that may also lead to nonconformity.

Sometimes, we have to shrug our shoulders, note the facts, and move on. It may not be economical to do anything other than that. In a line from *Forrest Gump*, a runner remarks to Gump that "Sh*t happens" and runs on.

The nature of the nonconformity is important to record, NOT what happens to it. Saying something is scrap may be convenient, but how it became so is vitally important to be recorded, along with where (in the process) and how many were affected, as a minimum. This requirement fundamentally affects the ability of the organization to define a problem and, thus, solve it.

One example demonstrates how off the rails this can go. A factory had been making molded plastic parts and scrapped off $600,000 of product in one year. Of course, this is a low estimate. In seeking to resolve the losses, a cross-functional team was assembled and used the 8D Problem Solving Method to determine the root cause and work on its removal. D2 is defining and being able to describe what the problem is and, with 15 people gathered around the table, it became abundantly clear that they were unable to define the problem.

There had been little analysis, evaluation, or testing of the reported defect. A list of eight actions that could be taken at almost zero cost to the company! As with many things in life, recognizing you have a problem is the first step in resolving it!

Performance Evaluation (9)

Monitoring, Measurement, Analysis, and Evaluation General (9.1.1)

Having established a QMS and set the relevant SMART objectives (OTIS) and controls in place for the various processes of the organization, it would be appropriate to perform measurements to confirm the product meets specifications and to see how the QMS is performing. As part of the PDCA cycle, this requirement of ISO 9001 can be 'checking' as a precursor to the 'act' of improvement.

The General requirements specify three basic areas of importance to be planned and implemented as measurement/monitoring activities, leading to the identification and action needed for improvement:

1. **Product** – to demonstrate conformity
2. **QMS** – to demonstrate conformity
3. **Continual improvement** – of the effectiveness of the QMS, linked to the objectives (performance) set for the processes (identified in 6.0)

Myth alert!

"All processes of the QMS need to be measured."

Myth busted!

The organization is free to choose what processes require measurement. Care should be taken not to overwhelm the reporting of process performance and, to some extent, limit those to customer-facing processes and those (directly) affecting product and, hence, cost. Although it might seem that measuring the time it takes to process a document change is important (to someone), it might be more appropriate to deal with that process by exception, rather than as the norm.

Myth alert!

"We have KPIs and they tell us what we need to measure."

Myth busted!

KPIs can, again, have the effect of overwhelming the reporting of process performance and certainly should be linked to SMART objectives first and foremost.

Monitoring and measuring is, for those who drive a vehicle, something we do each time we take a trip. Drivers use the information on the dashboard of their car to help them. Let's review what information is provided to get a sense of monitoring and measuring and why it is important:

- **Speed**

  The speed of the car should be monitored and measured. Why? Because it is a law that drivers must comply with on any given journey. If you don't pay attention, you'll be fined!

- **Fuel**

  It is normal to monitor the amount of fuel used during a journey to ensure it doesn't run out! We may be interested in the amount of fuel used to ensure that the vehicle is obtaining a certain specific fuel economy, is running properly, etc.

- **Engine condition**

  Either through the use of the rev. counter, which indicates the speed the engine is turning, or from the coolant temperature, we can tell something of the running conditions of the engine. However, we never need to know the values of, say, the coolant, which is normal at about 74 degrees Fahrenheit. Knowing the value isn't important, which is why most temperature gauges show only 'C' or blue for cold, 'N' or green for normal ,or 'H' or red for hot. The temperature values at these positions on the gauge aren't of interest, per se, but the position in the range is for monitoring purposes.

- **Tire pressures**

  Modern cars are fitted with tire pressure monitoring of some kind. These can flash a warning when loss of air is detected. They monitor a parameter that is related to the loss of air pressure, not actually measuring the pressure.

There are many other values that can be used to indicate that an engine is performing correctly: oil pressure, inlet vacuum, oil temperature, for example. Other values could be taken from the ancillary equipment on the engine, like the voltage and current from the generator, battery condition, and ignition dwell angle, etc.

Indeed, the modern Formula 1 racing car has thousands of measurements made every second of hundreds of parameters to give the engineers a total picture of just about everything the car is doing in response to the driver's control inputs. But then, the objectives – and costs – of running a Formula 1 racing car are totally different to that of driving an everyday road car.

We can also see that if all these values were to be presented to us as the driver, we would soon be overwhelmed. Indeed, some of these values are only of use if we are diagnosing a problem.

By keeping an eye on the basics, speed and fuel, most drivers can ensure they will complete their journey objectives: on time (speed over distance), on cost (fuel used), and without penalty (speeding ticket).

If we take this analogy in the context of the organization's QMS, when it comes to measurement and monitoring of products and processes, it is important to consider any statutory or regulatory requirements that may affect the products and processes (product regulations in the medical device world, for example). In lieu of these, the customer is next in line when it comes to identifying what is important to measure/monitor.

Identification of key features and characteristics of products is very common in many markets – automotive customers, for example, will identify classes of features on their product specifications, in terms of product safety (handed down from them through the supply chain), appearance, and fit/function, for example.

Customer Satisfaction (9.1.2)

Often thought of as a goal or an objective of the organization, its customers' level of satisfaction with the performance of the QMS is a useful indicator that the Standard doesn't require to be measured. Customer satisfaction is strongly linked to the effectiveness of the organization's ability to plan and control its processes to meet what it understands as the needs and expectations identified in the Context (section 4).

Myth alert!

"Customer satisfaction surveys must be sent."

"Customers are satisfied if they order more and don't make complaints."

"We get a supplier scorecard, so we're doing OK."

"Customers keep buying from us, so we don't need to survey them."

"We rarely get complaints; we must be doing things right."

Myth busted!

If an organization is serious about quality, it makes sense to ask the customer(s) what they think. Careful review of this requirement shows that it is not customer satisfaction, per se, that is to be obtained, monitored, and analyzed, but information relating to the customer's perception of whether their needs and expectations had been fulfilled.

As we know, it is often the unspoken comments of a customer that tell the most about their satisfaction. As you leave a restaurant, it is not unusual to be asked if everything was alright. Replies are sometimes a simple "yes, fine," when in fact there was more that could have been said to have solicited a fuller picture of the customer's level of satisfaction.

This requirement is also strongly linked to the organization's quality policy and objectives. In that section, we discussed whether it was truly intended to meet and exceed customer expectations, especially since expectations are not always communicated.

In a real-life situation, an organization approached significant customers (by highest sales revenue, product volume, etc.) and identified the key (customer) representatives:

- Purchasing
- Logistics
- Quality
- Engineering

The top manager would make a short call and ask if the price of their products was acceptable, if the delivery/packaging was acceptable, and if the quality of the product also met their requirements. Each of the first three customer representatives expressed their satisfaction. However, the engineering representative stated: "'You don't love us!" Further discussion revealed that the engineers were uncertain if their choice of product (selected from an online catalog) was correct in their chosen application. In short, the sales engineers were not visiting to participate in the design reviews, etc. – easily remedied!

Naturally, having given the organization their feedback, it is highly likely that customers will expect the organization to take action!

Internal Audits (section 9.2)

The requirement for Internal Audits seems to have been the subject of a significant quantity and variety of myths over the years. This is due, in part, to the lack of prior knowledge or experience of what a QMS audit is like. Some organizations may have been subjected to customer or regulatory body audits, but these are by nature external audits and, as such, cannot be relied upon as an appropriate model for setting up and running an effective internal audit program. Add to this the fact that most of the training and publications on the topic of ISO 9001 internal audits are based upon this model of external auditing and often drawing heavily on ISO 19011 – the ISO guidelines for management systems auditing – and so the resulting internal audits tend to be a bit like putting a square peg in a round hole. The focus, timing, methods, etc. of internal audits are, in many ways, substantially different to those of external audits.

Myth alert!

"You must cover all the ISO clauses once a year/every three years."

Myth busted!

There are no such requirements, except to say that a certification body may embody this in its contract with the organization – so read the small print when signing up for the certification service. In fact, when internal audits are planned and performed effectively, the QMS is covered in far less time.

Myth alert!

"One or two internal audits per year is sufficient."

Myth busted!

If consideration is given to the importance of the processes of the QMS and also changes, it can be seen that planning based on these will likely lead to more audits being performed in a year.

Myth alert!

"Audit findings should be graded as major, minor, or OFI."

Myth busted!

Grading of audit findings is a wholly external audit technique and is best avoided. The content of the audit report and nature of the findings should make it clear to those involved how serious the issue needs to be taken.

Myth alert!

"An audit calendar is required to show what is going to be audited in the coming year."

Myth busted!

The word 'frequency' seems to most to translate to a schedule of audit events throughout a year – which isn't what is required. In certain situations, there may well be a scheduling component that relates to an annual calendar – perhaps a plant shutdown, when maintenance occurs, or production activities related to harvesting fruit, vegetables, or grains. These would certainly be taken into consideration when scheduling an internal audit.

Myth alert!

"Auditors must be chosen from another department from the one they audit, so they are independent."

Myth busted!

Independence has, like many words in the English language, a variety of meanings. A quick look through a thesaurus reveals synonyms such as 'freedom,' 'impartiality,' etc. Sadly, since third-party certifiers and their auditors are independent (they don't directly represent the certified organization or the customers thereof), this alternative version of the state of independence has been taken as the model – hence it is often suggested that internal auditors cannot be involved in the process they are auditing. Prior versions of ISO 9001 stated that auditors "shall not audit their own work," which in very small organizations can be a practical impossibility. The further an auditor is from the process they audit is frequently justified as being a fresh set of eyes looking for improvements.

Myth alert!

"Someone must be a certified lead Auditor."

Myth busted!

As odd as it may seem, there are no formal qualifications required to be an internal auditor. This may seem to be a paradox when, in fact, one of the highest subscribed training courses related to ISO 9001 is the lead auditor course. Initially created to meet a demand for competent supplier QA personnel, this course became the de facto way to view what the certification body auditor would be doing for those organizations approaching ISO certification. Since many such courses were also offered by certification bodies, it was seen as a golden ticket to an organization being certified by its certification body of choice.

Myth alert!

"Auditors must have a checklist of questions."

Myth busted!

Checklists are both a blessing and a curse to the effectiveness of audits. While many auditors focus on the checklist and its use, the real benefit comes in the audit planning, which results in a document to be used by the auditor to guide them. If we take a simple analogy, it would be a shopping list, created to do the following:

- Ensure the trip to the store is successful
- Keep us from forgetting anything
- Organize the shopping process and help time keeping
- Help avoid bias, i.e. buying things we had no real use for (don't grocery shop when hungry!)
- Give evidence of planning so the task is completed

Top tips

It is the creation of the checklist that has most value and each auditor should prepare their own. Canned or preprinted checklists – especially those that can be found on the Internet and comprise the ISO 9001 requirements – turned into questions represent little value to auditor preparation and, hence, the effectiveness of the internal audits.

Internal audits are one of the requirements of ISO 9001 that are not 'institutional' to the way an organization works. Some form of audit is a familiar practice to most organizations, although it is often from a financial perspective or, as has been discussed above, through being evaluated by a customer or regulatory body. Since internal audits are required and, as we know, external 'certification' of compliance is not necessarily a goal for an organization that uses ISO 9001, what is the purpose of including these audits in the Standard?

Naturally, verification of compliance of the organization's QMS with the ISO 9001 standard is a given. The organization must determine that its QMS meets the requirements of ISO 9001, as long as management requires it. But that is often where the use of internal audits starts and stops. Let's see why.

It is not uncommon that internal audits begin with sending someone on an auditor training course. This is a great way to get started on the basics of an audit. The agenda for most courses will cover the fundamentals of planning, preparing, conducting, and reporting audits.

A typical internal auditor training course can (typically) be two or three days (16 – 24 hours), and a lead auditor course is typically 32 – 36 hours. Many courses are even accredited, which means they are recognized as being designed and delivered following the requirements of the ISO Guidelines on Management Systems Auditing, ISO 19011.

Once trained, it is tempting for the new auditor to create a checklist or an audit schedule or calendar that shows what is intended to be audited in the coming year. An organization cannot be successful if it requires certification of its QMS without having first implemented internal audits. In the run-up to the certification audit, the focus of the internal audit program is to ensure that no significant issues are found by the certification body auditor. This is further detailed in the chapter on certification. To accomplish this goal, it is often sufficient to simply do audits, armed with the ISO 9001 requirements turned into questions and some evidence – usually auditors' notes and audit nonconformity reports – to jump that hurdle. Sadly, the bar is, in many cases, set very low.

Once the organization's QMS is found to be in compliance and certified, the internal audits should be managed to a higher level and to ensure that the focus changes to bring another value to the organization beyond simple compliance with the ISO standard. To do this, the scheduling of audits must be changed from a 'push' system, where audits are scheduled to an annual 'calendar,' to one of a 'pull' or demand system, where they are scheduled according to management's needs for the business.

The ISO 9001 requirements for internal audits (9.2.2) state that the organization shall conduct internal audits at planned intervals to provide information on whether the QMS:

- Conforms to the organization's own requirements
- Conforms to the requirements of the Standard
- Is effectively implemented and maintained

This requirement gives us opportunities to consider that all processes are not created equally, that some might need to be audited as a priority and possibly more frequently than others. So, how can an audit program meet these requirements and be value-added to an organization?

Let's consider what is meant by the status of the processes of the QMS. Status might include something being new and/or changed, performing below or above expectations. Having something new or changed in relation to the following is also frequently associated with causing problems:

- Customers and requirements
- Suppliers
- Technology
- Regulations
- Process requirements
- Materials, equipment, etc.

The above are normally considered risks to the business. In fact, how many of us have heard that it's not a good idea to buy a new model car or similar until after it's been on the market for a year – to 'work out the bugs'?

Likewise, a process not performing to expectations, causing scrap, rework, and downtime – in fact any kind of waste – is also a risk. Got a process that exceeded its goal? Better find out why! Once the reason has been discovered, it could be used to improve other, similar processes.

In some cases, these are planned situations – including the new and changed aspects. Some, like poor performance, are unplanned. What could be done to prioritize an audit of a new, changed, or poorly performing process? This is where the importance of that process must be considered. We have to ask whether the process is important to meeting:

- Customer needs and expectations
- Regulatory compliance
- Costs

The importance of the process to the customer or other aspects of business can be considered as the impact of that process on the business.

It is common for internal audit programs to be developed on an annual calendar that predicts which aspects of the QMS are going to be audited. Often the objectives for developing the schedule are to ensure that the entire system is audited in that year, or to ensure all the ISO requirements are covered, etc. However, since there is no requirement to perform audits in that way, these internal audits often miss critical processes when they become an issue.

In one company, interns were recruited to cover on an assembly line during summer vacation time, which resulted in almost predictable product quality problems. The internal audit schedule forced the auditors to focus on features of the management system that were rarely problematic – instead of taking a critical look at the training and competency of the new people.

Imagine the hapless line supervisor having to act like a mother hen to their new operators while attempting to answer auditors' questions about product labeling, document control, etc.! Had the audit schedule directed the auditors to the training process when it was being implemented, it is highly likely to have diagnosed the problem with the process and attracted management's support for corrective actions.

An annualized calendar forces audits of processes that are either not a high priority or before/after any problems transpire, instead of helping to identify what contemporary actions need to be taken to improve things. No wonder, then, that in many organizations, the internal audit program is not well supported! Internal audits should be scheduled using current process performance data, feedback from customers, etc. to ensure that auditors are focused on what is on management's radar.

Internal audit management programs scheduled based on risk and impact can help usher in a new era, synonymous with risk assessment and continual improvements, rather than something done simply for compliance. Furthermore, the role of the auditor becomes elevated in status similar to that of a Six Sigma/Kaizen practitioner. Improving the internal audit program in this manner will help to ensure a domino effect on corrective actions and the management reviews of the QMS as a whole.

The selection of people to be auditors is made on the basis of finding someone who is independent of the process being audited. Someone from manufacturing can audit purchasing, someone from sales gets to audit design engineering, someone from customer service can audit sales.

Although it is important to maintain impartiality of auditors, this is one technique that a certification body employs which can be successfully mimicked. Certification body auditors are qualified by industry code (EAC/NACS, etc.), which means, in broad terms, they have experience in that sector or industry. So, why not consider that internal auditors should have a passable knowledge of the process/function they are assigned to audit?

Although many will say internal audits are a process and should be measured, experience tells us that there are no meaningful metrics to show they are effective. Some have suggested that the number of nonconformities, or conformity to an audit schedule, is a measure of internal audits; however, what is a 'good number' of audit nonconformities? 1 or 10? Indeed, since the requirement appears in the measurement and monitoring section of the ISO 9001 standard, audits are themselves, part of measuring and monitoring. The best we can hope for is that the organization's management takes an active, leadership role in deciding what and where internal audits should be performed.

Management Review (9.3)

Another requirement of ISO 9001:2015 – and its predecessors – that has failed to be realized for the benefit it provides is that of management review of the organization's QMS. While there may not be a lot of myths about it, those strike at the fundamentals of the purpose, participation, and timing of the review.

Myth alert!

"Management review has to be a meeting."

"It is the quality manager's job to present the review."

"One review per year is all that's needed."

"We have weekly/monthly quality meetings – they are our management review."

"We have to cover the whole of the inputs every time."

Myth busted!

Management review of the implementation of the effectiveness of the QMS is supposed to consider the following:

- Status of actions from previous reviews
- Changes in the internal and external issues (from section 4)
- Information on the performance and effectiveness of the QMS including:
  - Customer satisfaction and feedback from interested parties
  - The extent to which quality objectives have been met
  - Process performance and product conformity
  - Nonconformities and corrective actions
  - Monitoring and measurement results
  - Audit results
  - The performance of external providers
  - The adequacy of resources
  - The effectiveness of actions taken to address risks and opportunities
  - Opportunities for improvement

One way to consider management reviews of the QMS is to think of them as a navigating exercise on board a vessel, like a yacht.

When starting out on a voyage, it is wise to have a plan (map) and objectives, a way to measure progress, clear responsibilities for the crew, someone in authority (a captain), and resources (trained crew, food, water, etc.)

available to support getting to the planned destination on schedule.

Once a course has been determined and plotted, everyone can go about their processes and tasks of sailing the yacht. To ensure that the voyage ends at the planned destination, it will be necessary for the captain to confirm that the vessel is still headed in the planned direction and that weather and tides haven't moved the yacht from the intended course. In addition, progress should be measured to ensure that the objectives of the voyage are kept in sight and still achievable. Consideration may also be given to the available resources and whether they are sufficient to support the objectives, too. Course corrections may be required, and speed adjustment may be necessary to ensure the journey is completed on time.

Clearly, consulting the map, or checking progress or even waiting until a destination is reached, would be ineffective in ensuring objectives were met; the correct destination may not be reached, resources may be expended before the voyage is completed, arrival may be delayed, and measurements taken during the voyage may not have been accurate.

Of course, at the end of the voyage, it would be helpful to take stock of the situation to see if there were any lessons to be learned. In addition, it would be very prudent to ensure that the plan is consulted at least once or twice while en route to discover any deviations, before they put the voyage in jeopardy. If the vessel is large enough for a crew, then it will be those with assignments (think process owners) who report on the status, the past performance to the objectives set, and any actions necessary.

The same applies to management's review of the QMS. Once a year is of no value; twice won't tell you too much more.

Quarterly would give opportunities to manage the performance of the processes, taking a timely look at the need for correction or improvements along the way. In fact, there is no need to schedule any review – simply plan them. An effective review of the QMS is the cornerstone to maintaining and improving its effectiveness and while a number of events a year may be planned, others may or may not be needed, when performance dictates.

The idea of reviewing all the inputs would be inappropriate too. Let's take the actions to address risk and opportunities. If this included, as an example the (biggest) risk of availability of skilled people, then if the organization addresses that risk by developing an apprenticeship program – typically lasting four years – a quarterly review is likely too frequent, and at the end of four years is too late! When indicators are green, a cursory review is appropriate. When some are yellow, then let's lift the lid and look at those. When a red status occurs, action is necessary, plus a review of those also affected, including the impacts on requirements such as corrective actions, customer satisfaction, and the internal audits.

Process owners should be able to describe their responsibilities for their process, performance to goals, how that's measured, and what actions are being taken to correct/improve that performance. In this scenario, the internal audits provide validation that the QMS is providing the necessary controls on the processes.

Improvement (10)

We now find the QMS at a point where improvements are required – after all, there is a good chance that something didn't work out as planned and, even if it did all go well, the organization probably cannot rest on its laurels.

It is, perhaps, notable that ISO 9001 treats nonconformity and improvement in the same requirement. It may need some cultural adjustment by the organization to consider that the idea of correcting nonconformity is improvement. Indeed, if the organization is in the automotive supply chain, it is generally recognized that if a process is not robust, capable, and in control, it isn't at the required status that will be ready for improvement! This is, in part, due to the need to establish the IQ, OQ, and PQ (discussed previously).

Myth alert!

"There is a difference between 'continuous' and 'continual' improvement."

"It is necessary to have a procedure for continual improvement."

Myth busted!

Although these words do not have the same meaning in the English language, for the purposes of applying the ISO standard, they can be considered simply different approaches to achieving the same objective.

The approach the organization adopts in implementing any improvement should be appropriate to its needs. For example, the Six Sigma methodology can be considered a project or breakthrough type of improvement. People trained and qualified as either black belts or green belts comprise a team of improvement specialists. They participate in a project, following the DMAIC (Define, Measure, Analyze, Improve, Control) steps or similar. Implementation of a Six Sigma project tends to take time to carry out, sometimes running into months, with periods of no improvement, often while the next opportunities are identified. As a result, a typical graph of improvements (measured in savings) over time might look like this step chart:

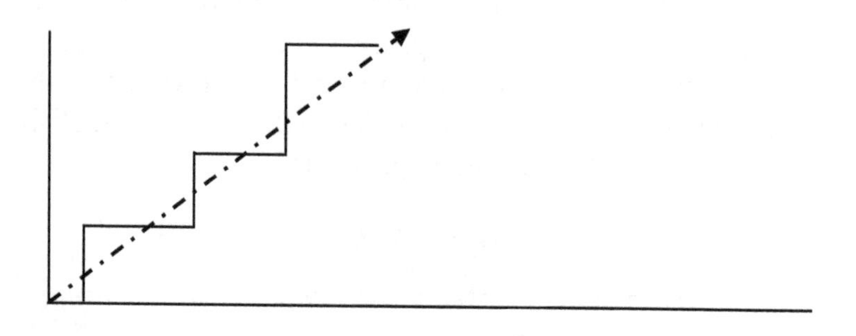

Figure 4: Graph of improvements

Improvements can also come from small-scale activities, such as the Kaizen events normally associated with the famous Toyota Production System or Lean manufacturing techniques. Kaizen is a Japanese word meaning "change for the better" and focuses on the reduction of waste. Improvement events are often characterized by small-scale events lasting one or two days, which happen regularly – often weekly or monthly. They can be represented by an (almost) straight line. We can see that the net result is the same, in terms of savings over a similar period.

CHAPTER 2: THE ISO GUIDANCE DOCUMENTS

As part of the family of ISO 9000 documents, ISO 9004 provides guidelines to those organizations seeking to implement the requirements specified in ISO 9001.

ISO 9004 is mentioned only once within the ISO 9001 requirements and only in the introduction – something that is rarely considered by implementers. This is borne out by the numbers of the individual volumes sold by ISO – at one point ISO 9001 outsold ISO 9004 by a factor of 10:1!

Those who did obtain a copy of ISO 9004 may not have been entirely satisfied with their acquisition! Let's briefly review the previous and current versions, since they are applicable to the ISO 9001 document that has remained substantially unchanged since the 2000 version.

ISO 9004:2018

This version of ISO 9004 is entitled "Quality management – Quality of an organization – Guidance to achieve sustained success."

The introduction states:

> "***Introduction***
>
> *This document provides guidance for organizations to achieve sustained success in a complex, demanding and ever-changing environment, with reference to the quality management principles described in ISO 9000:2015. Where they are applied collectively, quality management*

principles can provide a unifying basis for an organization's values and strategies.

While ISO 9001:2015 focuses on providing confidence in an organization's products and services, this document focuses on providing confidence in the organization's ability to achieve sustained success.

Top management's focus on the organization's ability to meet the needs and expectations of customers and other relevant interested parties provides confidence in achieving sustained success. This document addresses the systematic improvement of the organization's overall performance. It includes the planning, implementation, analysis, evaluation and improvement of an effective and efficient management system.

Factors affecting an organization's success continually emerge, evolve, increase or diminish over the years, and adapting to these changes is important for sustained success. Examples include social responsibility, environmental and cultural factors, in addition to those that might have been previously considered, such as efficiency, quality and agility; taken together, these factors are part of the organization's context.

The ability to achieve sustained success is enhanced by managers at all levels learning about and understanding the organization's evolving context. Improvement and innovation also support sustained success.

> *This document promotes self-assessment and provides a self-assessment tool for reviewing the extent to which the organization has adopted the concepts in this document (see Annex A).*"[3]

The guidance was published with the intention of being consistent with ISO 9001 – the term "consistent pair" being used to describe them both. The format of the ISO 9004 document was closely aligned to the ISO 9001 requirements so that cross-referencing was made easier.

ISO/TS 9002

ISO 9004 was never intended to be a how-to guide for those who were new to the concepts and practice of QMSs, which would be frustrating, especially when the title states "guidelines."

It did, however, provide excellent descriptions for those who sought to improve the basics of the QMS they had constructed, in particular concerning internal audit planning.

---

[3] *www.iso.org/obp/ui/#iso:std:iso:9004:ed-4:v1:en*.

CHAPTER 3: IMPLEMENTATION – A HOW-TO GUIDE

Once an organization has committed to implement a QMS based on ISO 9001, often the question arises: How? From what's been described in earlier chapters, it should be clear that implementation of a QMS in compliance with the requirements of ISO 9001 isn't simply 'say what you do, do what you say' or documenting a set of manuals, procedures, and work instructions to suit the requirements of the Standard.

Commonly asked questions voiced by those new to ISO 9001 implementation include, "How long does it take?," "What does it cost?," and "We've been in business for a long time, what else have we got to do to meet ISO?"

If we look at a tried and trusted methodology and describe the typical activities as well as key milestones involved to the point where the organization is ready to become certified, it will help any organization to answer – or at least estimate – what its particular implementation needs would be. If we take an analogy from the new product development process – the processes in which an organization launches a new product into the marketplace – we find that there are distinct similarities.

The phases and key action items and milestones can be represented diagrammatically, as shown on the following pages:

NEEDS ASSESSMENT (ALSO KNOWN AS A GAP ANALYSIS)

PLANNING AND PREPARATION

SYSTEM DESIGN AND DOCUMENTATION

SYSTEM IMPLEMENTATION AND AUDIT

SYSTEM REVIEW AND IMPROVEMENT

(The third-party certification process is covered in the following chapter.)

PHASE 5 – SYSTEM REVIEW AND IMPROVEMENT

Management review

Corrective action and improvement plans

Revised risks and opportunities

PHASE 4 – SYSTEM IMPLEMENTATION AND AUDIT

Process implementation

Product and process measurement and monitoring

Customer feedback

Results analysis

Internal audit

PHASE 3 – SYSTEM DESIGN AND DOCUMENTATION

QMS scope established

Process of the QMS identified, inputs, outputs, controls, criteria, etc.

Sequence and interaction established

Documented information identified – 'maintained' and 'retained' types

PHASE 2 – PLANNING AND PREPARATION

Competency/training requirements defined

Process ownership established

Detailed action list/timeline for implementation

Responsibilities and authorities defined

Quality policy and quality objectives established

Communications plan created

Budget and resource plan

SWOT analysis (context and interested parties)

PHASE 1 – GAP ANALYSIS

Three types of gap identified

Management commitment

ISO debriefing/overview session

Draft quality policy, quality objectives

Phase 1 – Gap analysis

Those organizations that decide to implement a QMS in compliance with ISO 9001 often have many of the requirements of the Standard in place – in some way, shape, or form simply through the needs of doing business and the innate ability of people to create processes, controls and documentation – for many reasons.

This fact, plus the commonly held belief (myth) that implementing ISO 9001 means "say (document) what you do, do what you say" (document), can lead organizations down the wrong path, leading to too much documentation being created, often in a format that is a bureaucracy to use and maintain.

Similarly, a 'desk analysis' may be performed, comparing what the organization has, in terms of 'paperwork' – only – against the ISO 9001 requirements. This can also give an incorrect view of the gap between what is required by the Standard and the organization's current situation, since it doesn't take into consideration actual practice and is, therefore, only a two-dimensional view of the QMS.

A fully effective gap analysis looks at the currently implemented practices of an organization in terms of:

- Something ISO 9001 requires that the organization practices, but may not be formal or fully compliant with the requirement
- Something ISO 9001 requires, and the organization isn't practicing the requirement
- Something ISO 9001 requires and, whether the organization has formally defined a process or not, the implementation is not fully effective

To determine the type and extent of these gaps, an audit may be undertaken by someone fully competent in understanding ISO 9001 and effective auditing techniques. This second aspect of competency is of vital importance, since the auditor will be evaluating undocumented processes, etc.

Frequently, organizations choose to contract a qualified consultant to perform the gap analysis, since they often possess the necessary skills and experience to carry out the audit, provide the report, and debrief management in the nature and extent of the gaps, as a prelude to the next phase, which involves planning for implementation. It is not uncommon for management to have a (brief) overview of ISO 9000, including the background of its development, ISO 9001 requirements, and the certification process, given by the consultant after the gap analysis audit is performed.

Throughout the management overview session, the findings from the gap analysis can be used as discussion points to better describe and explain what is required by the Standard and, if appropriate, to begin the creation of a detailed action plan. Some form of visual metaphor or graphic can be used to help effectively convey the state of compliance with ISO 9001, giving the organization's management a clear picture, for example:

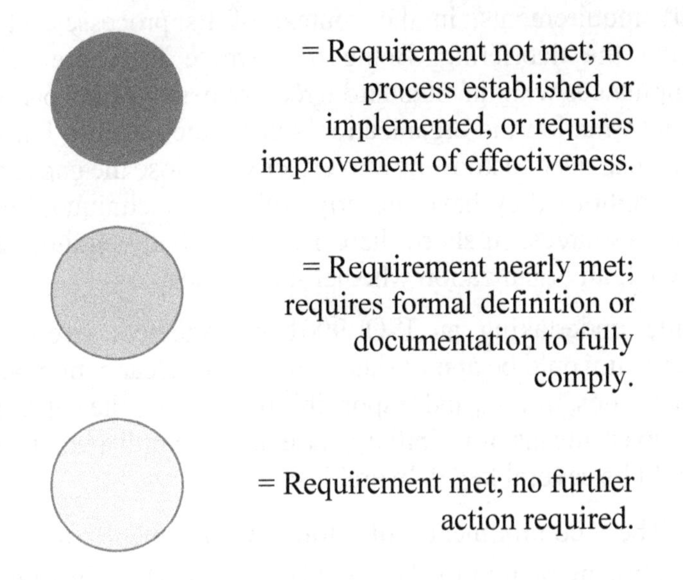

By way of a caution, it has been known to engage the services of an ISO 9000 certification body to perform this gap analysis, for many reasons. Its auditors should, after all, be familiar with the requirements of ISO 9001. Experience shows that this is not the most effective path to take, since the rules of accreditation restrict the certification body from consulting – including the delivery of on-site or in-house training at a client organization.

If the gap analysis is performed by someone different to the person who leads the management overview training event, the gap analysis report contents may be difficult to interpret. This, in turn, may result in discussions not being based on the fullest understanding of the actual practices.

Furthermore, since an IAF-accredited certification body cannot provide consultation services, the organization may not get the fullest benefit from its understanding of the ISO

9001 requirements, in the context of its processes, etc., during the debriefing. Being told where there are non-compliances with the Standard's requirements is only part of the information the organization's personnel need to know. They also need to know how to effectively close the gaps and what options they have, in terms of tools, techniques, and other resources. In short, the certification body auditor can only tell an organization whether it complies.

While undertaking an ISO 9001 management overview course, it would be appropriate to develop a clear action plan of activities, timing, and responsibilities to close the gaps. By whatever means this initial phase is accomplished, there should be several key deliverables:

- The commitment of top management to the implementation of the organization's QMS – including the commitment to budget, timing, and personnel resources to support implementation
- A communications plan – what this means to the organization, the roles people will be playing, the time frame, descriptions of what is going to be new/different and how it affects people, for example internal audits, the purpose of ISO 9001 certification, and the process (if electing to become certified)

Phase 2 – Planning and preparation

The successful implementation of a QMS will require a detailed project plan of tasks, deliverables, responsibilities, and duration/timing. For each of the subsequent phases, the organization must ensure that all gaps previously identified are broken down into assignable activities with a clear result. By constructing a clear plan, there is a greater likelihood of management being able to set clear expectations, monitor progress, and address roadblocks. Furthermore, a better understanding of the duration and total resources required can be identified, which may translate to accurate budgeting and associated expenditure controls. In this phase, it is advisable for top management to be ascribed to 'process ownership.' Although the terminology isn't found in ISO 9001:2015, the "Leadership" section can be seen to describe the role of "process owners" and, indeed, it is often a default situation for an organization to have a member of personnel hold responsibility in practice.

A simple project plan can be created as an Excel or Smartsheets file or similar, which can be an effective tool.

Whatever format is chosen, the plan for the creation and implementation of the QMS should clearly define:

- The person(s) responsible for accomplishing the task(s)
- The duration of the task(s)
- The deliverable(s) associated with the task(s)
- The timing of the task(s) relative to others
- A clear indication of the task(s) that are related (feed) or result from others, in a logical sequence

As each task is completed (or not), progress can be tracked, using traffic light (R/Y/G) status indicators. Those that fall into yellow (behind schedule) or red (stalled) status can be brought to the attention of management for understanding and resolution.

Frequent reviews should be undertaken by the personnel involved in the implementation to ensure the plan is kept updated and that any unforeseen activities are added, with the appropriate assignments, etc. As progress is made, the reviews will morph as each phase is undertaken.

Furthermore, it is possible to eventually transition the implementation project reviews into a platform for the management reviews required by ISO 9001.

On completion of the plan, approval should be gained from top management to proceed.

Phase 3 – System design and documentation

This phase is remarkably like the design and development phase for a product. The design of the QMS documentation is, in many ways, like a product. ISO 9001:2015 has almost no requirements in this regard and leaves it to the organization to determine what "maintained documented information" is required. This may include a consideration of the interested parties identified in the Context of the Organization section and the need to retain organizational knowledge, which is required in section 7.

The QMS documentation must be planned and have competent people to create it, and consideration must be given to how requirements that are applicable are going to be incorporated. Once designed, the documentation must be produced and assembled.

Good product design is also generally accepted to be something that is handed over to the people who are tasked with making it in a seamless manner. The design outputs are understood, well defined, and meet any applicable regulatory requirements, and, most importantly, can be implemented – or made – without causing problems. It is therefore important to involve the people who make the product to ensure requirements are defined in a way that makes life easy for them, by soliciting their input.

Rarely, and unfortunately, this comparison is never fully made, with the result that documentation causes problems for the people who have to use it. It has been stated, previously, that more attention is given to tiers or levels of documentation, or to the format, and to laying out things by ISO clause, than to the veracity of the information contained in the document.

It is of vital importance that the people who do the work contribute to the creation of whatever documents are really needed to perform work. It is often the case that having created a document describing how some work is to be carried out, it is 'thrown over the wall' to the supervisor to ensure training is carried out.

In creating documentation for the QMS, a good starting point is to inventory all and every existing document. Because these are documents that people find useful – even if not perfect – they can be used when completing another important step.

Mapping the processes of the organization is a very revealing part of the creation of the QMS and its documentation. Process mapping should be performed by those members of staff who are involved with each individual process, including the process owner, internal 'supplier,' and 'customer', facilitated by an impartial person. This person is primarily there to ensure that no one person takes a lead in describing the process, to ensure that the existing process is captured, warts and all. Capturing the process 'as is' is significant because opportunities to improve what happens often become obvious, particularly if care is taken to identify waste.

It is tempting to 'flow chart' a process, using the type of flow diagram used in determining the logic behind early computer programming. Apart from anything else, such a technique captures only what the 'logic' is, not what actually happens.

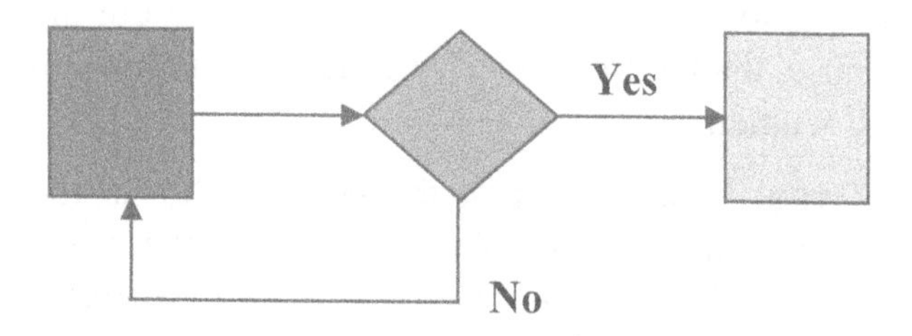

Figure 5: Flow chart

As discussed previously regarding the format of documentation, more effort may be wasted on the shape of the elements of the flow chart and their relative meaning, rather than gathering information on the actual process, possibly to the overall detriment of the result.

Capturing each process in its rough form can be best achieved by papering a wall of a meeting room, and having a team draw free form, using markers, sticky notes, postcards, etc.

Using examples of the existing documents that have been inventoried, the process maps can be populated. As issues are detected, consideration may be given to the contribution of any documents. For example, if a purchasing requisition form is used, but it is not clear how much information is needed – as a minimum – the buyer who receives it may have to halt the process, causing delays, etc. This should become apparent and a change made to the form design or a clear instruction given on what the minimum criteria are to be.

Once captured in rough form, consideration can be given to the final format for documents. With networked computers and applications such as Word, Adobe Acrobat and Microsoft Visio, the creation and structuring of the QMS documentation can be logically defined. Care should be taken, however, to ensure a convention for the naming of files and folders. When public access drives are used for QMS documentation, controls should be put in place to limit dumping of miscellaneous files, etc.

Furthermore, the controls necessary to allow access to read, without unauthorized editing, are also relatively straightforward to accomplish. One consideration is that unless all personnel who participate in the QMS have access to a computer/tablet to the documentation, some form of hard copy documentation may still be required by those people.

At some point in the development of the documented QMS, it will be important to put down the pens and begin the fourth phase.

Phase 4 – System implementation and audit

For a proportion of the processes, it will be business as usual, since the creation of the QMS has merely formalized what was already in place and working well.

For those other aspects of the QMS that are new or even substantially changed – reference back to the gap analysis results – it may be necessary to identify new or additional competencies. As has been stated previously, it isn't absolutely necessary to train people on everything new or different. What should be established is whether anyone involved in performing a process – or part of it – is required to possess any additional/different competencies.

An example of a knee-jerk conclusion being drawn – which results in training – is when identifying candidates to become internal quality system auditors. While it may be obvious to suggest that most organizations have no one who possesses the necessary skills and experience as an internal auditor, sending a handful of people on a two-, three-, or even five-day auditor training course may not result in all the appropriate competencies being developed. At best, such training permits only a very basic level of audit skills.

Consideration must be given to some other basic or entry-level criteria for auditor candidates, onto which the auditor skills may be built. Even fundamental communications skills are often overlooked, as are interpersonal or soft skills, and even knowledge of the purpose and operation of other functions of the organization. The Standard on auditing, ISO 19011, gives excellent descriptions of characteristics auditors should possess.

When the processes of the QMS are demonstrating results, it will be necessary to perform internal audits.

As has been established, there are many and varied myths surrounding establishing and implementing an internal audit program. When faced with determining what and when to audit the organization's newly minted QMS, there is a clue in the requirements of the ISO 9001 standard, 9.2.2. This states, in part, *"that an audit programme (a number of audits) be planned, taking into consideration the importance of the processes..."* Substituting 'performance' for 'importance,' we can develop an understanding of where and what to audit as a priority. In the context of the QMS, we can take risk as being higher with a process that doesn't perform as planned and that makes it important if there is an impact on customers, regulatory compliance, or the cost of scrap, rework, etc. In the run-up to a certification audit, it would be entirely appropriate to select those processes/areas/activities of the QMS that are new to the organization, have been changed, and have a potential impact on customer satisfaction.

Phase 5 – System review and improvement

Following the period of implementation and auditing of the QMS, a point is reached when there is sufficient data regarding the performance of the processes. The next key milestone is to prepare and perform a review by the organization's management.

From the performance data of the processes, it will be necessary to analyze this for trends, etc. This should be performed by the process owners, including the identification of corrective and improvement actions.

Despite ISO 9001 not requiring a meeting to perform a review by management of the QMS, experience has shown that this method brings a number of benefits. In many situations, the results of the internal audit process are not well understood as a review item. Since the internal audit process, for example, is new to the organization, it is common for the review to go through a detailed analysis of the findings, etc. without looking at what they really mean.

By looking at the following matrix, we can see that internal audit results can be viewed as validation of the QMS being effective in producing process results. Although a clear set of review topics is defined in ISO 9001, what is often missing is a '30,000-feet view' of the QMS as a management tool to deliver results.

Table 1: Management Review in a Nutshell

PROCESS PERFORMANCE	INTERNAL AUDIT RESULTS	ACTIONS REQUIRED
Meets or exceeds targets set	QMS being followed	Improvement of QMS?
Meets or exceeds targets set	QMS NOT being followed	Improve QMS in line with practice
Below targets set	QMS being followed	Corrective action required on process
Below targets set	QMS NOT being followed	Corrective action on QMS

Each process owner brings their analysis of their process performance, objectives, and action items to present and discuss with the other process owners.

From the review, opportunities to improve some aspect of the QMS should be weighed and the appropriate resources identified and assignments made to roll out the approved actions.

One of the outcomes of holding a review of the QMS is to confirm the readiness to undertake the certification audit. When all process owners can confirm they know their process performance, and have taken actions to correct and improve some aspect of the QMS, and that (importantly) the internal audits have validated the use of the QMS in controlling the processes to achieve results, the organization is substantially ready to undergo the stage 1 certification audit.

Once certified, the review of the QMS will be substantially similar, but part of the review will take into consideration the preparation for and results from subsequent certification body audits.

Once an organization achieves certification of its QMS, the focus should be turned from the basic implementation needs and toward maintenance and improvement. By referring back to the PDCA cycle diagram, we can see that the organization can employ key activities of the QMS in directing the maintenance and improvements required.

As stated previously, management review of the QMS is the cornerstone of the maintenance and improvement.

CHAPTER 4: QUALITY – JUST WHAT IS IT?

It is appropriate to understand some basics that underpin the reason for the Standard being in existence. Since ISO 9000 has in its title the word "Quality," defining 'quality' is important to understanding the context of a QMS. It is a word that can be a slippery concept to grasp.

There are all manner of definitions or descriptions of 'quality' – some conceptual, some esoteric, and some reasonably accurate. Definitions include "Doing it right first time" and "Selling products that don't come back, to customers who do," but for the purposes of understanding the Standard, we should look to the definition that is found in the "normative reference" for ISO 9001: the vocabulary document known as ISO 9000:

> *"degree to which a set of inherent characteristics fulfils requirements"*

This definition is a classical one, but may be less than helpful to those who are new to the concept. Therefore, for the purposes of understanding this book, and the application of ISO 9001 to an organization, 'quality' is considered as:

> *"Doing what your customer tells you they want."*

No surprises, changes, or late or early deliveries: What they want, delivered on time. Simple, really!

Furthermore, it is going to be very necessary that the organization's management has a clear and consistent understanding of this definition, because, without it, the rest of the implementation of the ISO 9001 requirements will be fundamentally flawed. The reasons will become clear later.

Furthermore, it is also important that key concepts which hinge on the use of the word 'quality' are also fully understood as distinct and separate – as well as being somewhat interrelated.

Those key concepts are:

- Quality control
- Quality assurance
- Quality management
- Total quality

Quality control – Or "you can't inspect quality into products!"

How 'quality' is achieved by an organization has been gradually changing since the Second World War, particularly with the trend to mass production techniques. It was traditional, in western manufacturing organizations, for quality control personnel – sometimes dressed in white lab coats – to inspect, check, and test products to see if they met the specification. Often, the most talented people from the manufacturing line were recruited to the quality control department, since they knew nearly everything about the manufacturing process; they also knew the problems that were manifest in the products. They were, simply, the best at finding the faults. This approach was costly and time consuming, and frustrated the people on the manufacturing line and their supervision. In some situations, the manufacturing departments would play games with the quality control people to meet production schedules and delivery dates, when products had been suspected of being rejects.

Worst of all, the quality control effort directed at the product wasn't very effective in preventing defects getting to customers. A common assertion is that even 100% inspection (by people) is only 80% effective, at best.

To demonstrate this ineffectiveness, a simple test of the power of observation is used, where the reader has to count the number of times the letter 'F' appears in the following sentence:

"FINISHED FILES ARE THE RESULT OF YEARS OF SCIENTIFIC STUDY COMBINED WITH THE EXPERIENCE OF YEARS..."
(Answer: 6)

Those who were alive during this era can often tell stories about their (or families') experiences of the defects that afflicted consumer products!

Quality control is still an aspect of ISO 9001, albeit not performed the way as previously described. All processes need control(s), which may include measurement of process parameters and/or product characteristics and prove conformity to a specification or 'quality.'

Quality assurance – Because assumptions are a poor choice!

Previously described in the Introduction, major purchasing organizations (mainly government entities such as departments of defense or food and drugs agencies) required suppliers to implement quality assurance programs. The requirements for these quality assurance programs were published in contractually binding documents that became the predecessors of ISO 9001.

The quality assurance program requirements emphasized that suppliers had to operate the basics for assuring the quality of the products they manufactured. These basics included having the supplier create and maintain:

- A quality assurance manual
- Documented procedures/work instructions
- Approved suppliers (list)
- Measuring equipment calibration
- Controls for a non-conforming product
- Training for personnel
- A quality manager/representative
- Inspection records
- Etc.

As the use of supplier quality assurance requirements (as they were known) became widespread, the top-level suppliers (tier 1, or primes) also started to pass them down through their supply chains. As a result, these lower-level suppliers were frequently required to implement and maintain a variety of quality assurance programs to meet each of their major customers' requirements. Frustratingly, although there was substantial similarity across these customer quality assurance requirements, the supplier organizations had to maintain separate programs and documentation! Indeed, as mentioned previously, one supplier in the UK familiar to the author created and maintained 14 distinct quality assurance manuals to satisfy this demand, despite the fact that the product was a proprietary design!

Quality management – Quality doesn't just happen!

In the closing years of the 20th century, there has been a gradual move toward the recognition that the achievement of 'quality' and customer satisfaction is one of the core purposes of any organization – whether that organization is for profit or not. With this recognition has come the understanding that management and control of the organization's processes is what delivers that quality, from the process of developing and offering a new product into a market, taking an order from a customer, through to the delivery of that product and any post-sales services that also may be offered. What was required of a supplier organization as quality assurance has been enhanced and expanded to include not only the processes and activities thar are closely associated with making a product but also those that support and enable those product-related processes. This approach to quality is known today as quality management.

We can consider the relative scopes of the three 'quality' practices in the following manner:

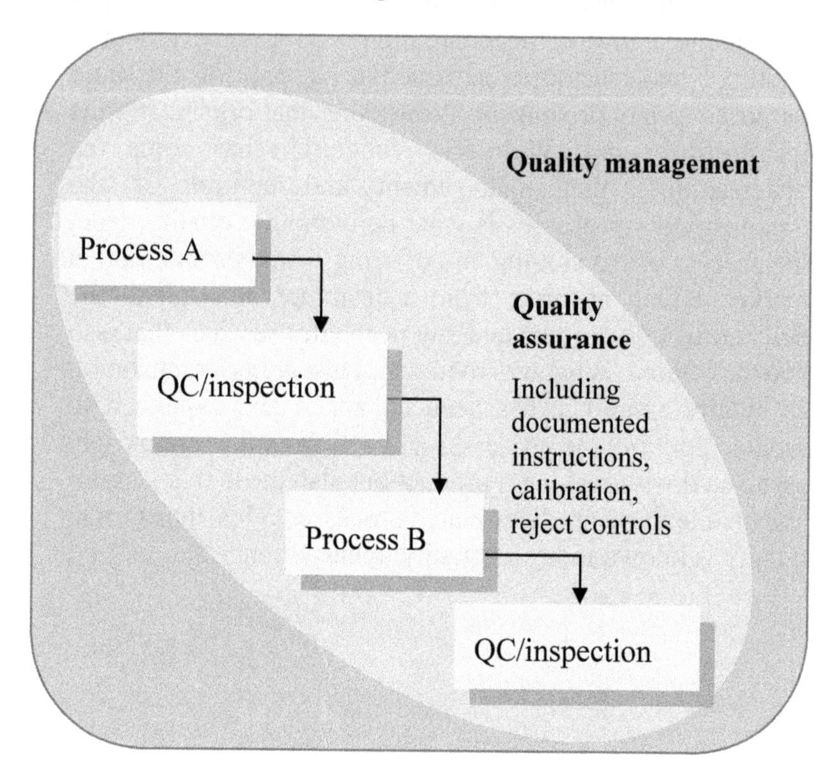

Figure 6: The three 'quality' practices

We can see that quality control activities have a very specific application, often to inspect the output from a process before the next process is carried out. Quality assurance often focuses on the elements that can also go to make the quality control work more effective, for example calibration of equipment and inspection instructions, similarly with the relationship between quality assurance and quality management.

The 'total quality' movement

Between 1950 and 1980, a number of quality 'gurus' came to prominence. Their work was based on the principles that inspecting quality into product isn't effective. These people shaped much of today's approaches to quality and what has become known as 'total quality management":

- Phillip Crosby
- Dr. W Edwards Deming
- Dr. Armand Feigenbaum
- Dr. Walter Shewhart
- Phillip Crosby, known in part for his *Quality Is Free* book, formulated the "Four Absolutes of Quality":
  1. Conformance to Requirements
  2. Right First Time
  3. Price of Non-conformance
  4. Prevention not Detection

Known as the father of modern quality, Dr. W Edwards Deming established many of the principles and practices of the contemporary approach to managing the (business) processes of an organization to produce a quality product. Deming is widely credited with leading the Japanese manufacturers in rebuilding their capabilities in the years after the Second World War. The adoption of Deming's management principles by notables such as Toyota, Honda, Sony, etc. has been credited as the reason they dominate their markets with high-quality products.

Often thought of as being the granddaddy of the total quality movement, Dr. Armand Feigenbaum conceived the idea of 'total quality control' (TQM). In addition to identifying the costs associated with getting quality wrong (as did Crosby),

Feigenbaum also highlighted the "hidden factory" – the name he gave to the extra work done in correcting quality problems.

Dr. Walter Shewhart's focus was on the use of statistics to control manufacturing processes. His understanding of process variations and the ability to use data was inspirational to Deming, who used this to formulate the widely used PDCA cycle, also known as the Shewhart Cycle. It is this PDCA cycle that forms the basis of the implementation diagram developed for ISO 9001:2015:

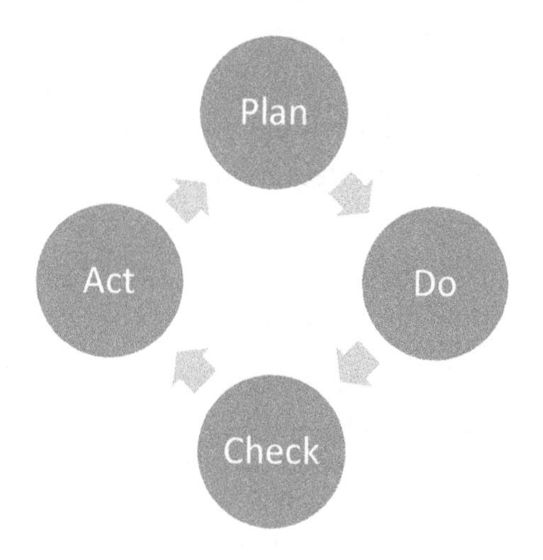

Figure 7: The PDCA cycle

It is often suggested that none of these thought leaders in total quality management would have supported the implementation of the original ISO 9000 requirements to assure a quality product. The current version may, however, not be so anathema to them, since in the years leading up to the release of the 2000 version, the ISO Technical Committee members did much to consider and formulate how total quality management concepts might be incorporated. Moving from quality assurance toward quality management made it necessary to adopt a more encompassing description of how quality and customer satisfaction are systematically and effectively achieved.

For example, the ISO 9001 standard encourages organizations to consider seven quality management principles (found in 0.2 of the Introduction) when implementing their QMS.

These principles are:

1. *Customer Focus*
2. *Leadership*
3. *Engagement of People*
4. *Process Approach*
5. *Improvement*
6. *Evidence-based Decision Making*
7. *Relationship Management*

If we look at Deming's 14 Principles, we'll see that those at the foundation of ISO 9000 are surprisingly similar:

1. *"Create constancy of purpose toward improvement of product and service, with the aim to become competitive and to stay in business, and to provide jobs.*
2. *Adopt the new philosophy. We are in a new economic age. Western management must awaken to the challenge, must learn their responsibilities, and take on leadership for change.*
3. *Cease dependence on inspection to achieve quality. Eliminate the need for inspection on a mass basis by building quality into the product in the first place.*

4. *End the practice of awarding business on the basis of price tag. Instead, minimize total cost. Move toward a single supplier for any one item, on a long-term relationship of loyalty and trust.*
5. *Improve constantly and forever the system of production and service, to improve quality and productivity, and thus constantly decrease costs.*
6. *Institute training on the job.*
7. *Institute leadership. The aim of supervision should be to help people and machines and gadgets to do a better job. Supervision of management is in need of overhaul, as well as supervision of production workers.*
8. *Drive out fear, so that everyone may work effectively for the company.*
9. *Break down barriers between departments. People in research, design, sales, and production must work as a team, to foresee problems of production and in use that may be encountered with the product or service.*
10. *Eliminate slogans, exhortations, and targets for the work force asking for zero defects and new levels of productivity. Such exhortations only create adversarial relationships, as the bulk of the causes of low quality and low productivity belong to the system and thus lie beyond the power of the workforce.*

11a. *Eliminate work standards (quotas) on the factory floor. Substitute leadership.*

11b. *Eliminate management by objective. Eliminate management by numbers, numerical goals. Substitute leadership.*

12a. Remove barriers that rob the hourly worker of his right to pride of workmanship. The responsibility of supervisors must be changed from sheer numbers to quality.

12b. Remove barriers that rob people in management and in engineering of their right to pride of workmanship. This means, inter alia, abolishment of the annual or merit rating and of management by objective.

13. Institute a vigorous program of education and self-improvement.

14. Put everybody in the company to work to accomplish the transformation. The transformation is everybody's job."[4]

Clearly, not all of Deming's principles were adopted! ISO 9001 still maintains objectives (12) for the QMS, but many of the seven quality management principles mentioned in ISO 9001 can be seen to be aligned with Deming's.

---

[4] https://deming.org/explore/fourteen-points/.

CHAPTER 5: ISO 9000 – A LEGEND IN ITS OWN LIFETIME?

Today, after 30 years of implementation and certification experiences all over the world, many myths and legends have grown and been promulgated surrounding the use of ISO 9000, including:

"Say what you do, do what you say" or

"ISO certification allows you to make concrete life jackets" (a similar quote was printed in USA Today in 1998).

Many of these myths have delayed managements' interest in using ISO 9000 as a tool to improve the way business operates, to drive the result that customers are satisfied with the results which, in turn, can lead to repeat business. Management can focus on reduced waste and higher efficiencies, through implementing an improved management system of processes and controls.

Today, Internet groups and forums are filled with questions and comments from users concerning all manner of ISO 9000-related issues. These posts show that many of the original myths and legends that began to pervade implementation of ISO 9000 requirements back in the 1990s are still alive and kicking today.

Perhaps a contributory factor in attracting so much misunderstanding of the purpose behind the Standard is that there was no model or other description of what a QMS should be when implemented.

Early versions of the ISO 9001 requirements heavily emphasized documented procedures for each of the 20 'elements' or clauses – which could easily be aligned to individual functions or departments – with the result that implementing organizations often built a QMS of paperwork for each function. In doing so, they often failed to address the quality problems resulting from interdepartmental 'dysfunction.' This silo approach was, in part, the reason for the "Say what you do, do what you say" myth.

In 2015, a diagrammatic description of the interaction of the requirements of the Standard was incorporated to facilitate an understand of their relationship to the Deming PDCA cycle.

In July 2009, the ISO and the IAF released a joint statement on the expected outcomes of ISO 9001 and accredited certification.

It states:

> *"Expected Outcomes for Accredited Certification to ISO 9001(from the perspective of the organization's customers)*
>
> *For the defined certification scope, an organization with a certified quality management system consistently provides products that meet customer and applicable statutory and regulatory requirements and aims to enhance customer satisfaction.*
>
> *Notes:*
>
> *a. "Products" also includes "services."*
>
> *b. Customer requirements for the product may either be stated (for example in a contract or an agreed specification) or generally implied (for example in the*

organization's promotional material, or by common practice for that economic/industry sector).

c. Requirements for the product may include requirements for delivery and post-delivery activities.

What (IAF) accredited certification to ISO 9001 means

To achieve conforming products, the accredited certification process is expected to provide confidence that the organization has a quality management system that conforms to the applicable requirements of ISO 9001. In particular, it is to be expected that the organization:

A. has established a quality management system that is suitable for its products and processes, and appropriate for its certification scope
B. analyzes and understands customer needs and expectations, as well as the relevant statutory and regulatory requirements related to its products
C. ensures that product characteristics have been specified in order to meet customer and statutory/ regulatory requirements
D. has determined and is managing the processes needed to achieve the expected outcomes (conforming products and enhanced customer satisfaction)
E. has ensured the availability of resources necessary to support the operation and monitoring of these processes
F. monitors and controls the defined product Characteristics
G. aims to prevent nonconformities, and has systematic improvement processes in place to:

1. Correct any nonconformities that do occur (including product nonconformities that are detected after delivery)
2. Analyze the cause of nonconformities and take corrective action to avoid their recurrence
3. Address customer complaints
H. has implemented an effective internal audit and management review process
I. is monitoring, measuring and continually improving the effectiveness of its quality management system.

What accredited certification to ISO 9001 does not mean

1) It is important to recognize that ISO 9001 defines the requirements for an organization's quality management system, not for its products. Accredited certification to ISO 9001 should provide confidence in the organization's ability to "consistently provide product that meets customer and applicable statutory and regulatory requirements". It does not necessarily ensure that the organization will always achieve 100% product conformity, though this should of course be a permanent goal.
2) ISO 9001 accredited certification does not imply that the organization is providing a superior product, or that the product itself is certified as meeting the requirements of an ISO (or any other) standard or specification."

The myth of the concrete life jackets is just that – a myth! Since in several of the preceding paragraphs there are many references to meeting statutory and regulatory requirements, as well as determining customers' needs and expectations, a concrete life jacket couldn't be designed, tested, and produced and be delivered to a customer. There are numerous regulations that require a life jacket to float – with an adult strapped into it – and product testing would have verified the ability of the jacket to float (in accordance with the regulations). These requirements would have been factored into a number of key requirements of ISO 9001 and would be necessary components of the life jacket manufacturer's QMS!

Many ISO pundits have promoted ISO 9001 as the model for business management without regard for the many functions of an organization that sustain it, outside of the QMS, including finance and marketing – neither of which are even alluded to in the Standard. Although many of the concepts and requirements in ISO 9001 can be found in practices adopted by other functions – for example, regular reviews of financial performance by management are a common occurrence in mature organizations, as are audits – in reality, ISO 9001 represents a very product-centric (or service-centric) set of processes, controls, etc.

CHAPTER 6: ISO 9000 AND THE FUTURE

Historically, the development of ISO 9001 goes through a cycle of review and revision that up until now, have taken some six to eight years to complete (1987 – 1994, 2000, 2008, 2015), so it is likely that the next version will not appear for at least another five years – according to ISO/TC 176. In the second quarter of 2021, the results of public polling and a feedback review resulted (by a narrow margin) in the decision to maintain the 2015 version, unchanged.

Despite ISO 9001 being intended as a 'one-size-fits-all' set of quality management requirements, some industry-specific supply chain documents have appeared, notably IATF 16949 (automotive industry) and AS9100, AS9110, and AS9120. The railway and petroleum industry also have theirs: IRIS and API Spec Q1. These are based on the ISO 9001 requirements (although are not, technically speaking, standards) and have industry-specific quality requirements, tools, and techniques woven throughout them. For example, as we know, ISO 9001 doesn't require a quality manual, but IATF 16949 makes it a requirement. AS9100D suggests that in documenting a number of the requirements – particularly from section 4, such as a list of interested parties – that the resulting compilation of documents might be called a quality manual…

The authors of the automotive IATF 16949 have 'decoupled' their supply chain quality management requirements from ISO 9001, citing the need for greater flexibility to amend industry-specific requirements. With the advent of autonomous vehicles, etc., the management of quality is likely to evolve rapidly. At the time of writing, it is not clear if other industries have plans to change their respective documentation.

Industry 4.0

In the past few years, the expression 'Industry 4.0' has found wider and wider recognition. In broad terms, it is a name applied to what is being described as the Fourth Industrial Revolution. There have been three previous disruptive events or technologies that have forever changed the industrial world, which we know as:

1. Steam power
2. Electricity
3. Computing

Industry 4.0 comprises the following nine classifications of technologies:

1. Cloud computing
2. Big data
3. Cybersecurity
4. Industrial Internet of Things (IIoT)
5. Augmented/virtual reality
6. Simulation
7. Additive manufacturing (3D printing)
8. Robotics
9. Systems integration

These technologies may be grouped relative to each other, for example:

- Cloud computing/big data/cybersecurity
- Robotics/IIoT/additive manufacturing/systems integration

- Augmented reality/simulation

Despite discussions around the topic of 'Quality 4.0,' there is as yet no authoritative understanding of how, when, or indeed if the ISO 9001 requirements may be impacted by the inevitable changes that must occur. With technologies enabling greater automation and, as a result, the reduction or even elimination of process and product variations, including errors made by humans, it might be seen that attaining quality may turn to (automated) inspection and verification activities. We know, for example, there are multiple checks placed on processing information when we make purchases from online markets, such as Amazon, eBay, and Etsy, which go a long way to error-proof the transactions.

Without a crystal ball, if quality can be controlled automatically, then perhaps the function of quality management will focus on the quality of the strategic direction and related planning by organizations and their ability to satisfy emerging opportunities. With that, the place of the quality profession will have moved from the very (back) end of the line to the front…

FURTHER READING

IT Governance Publishing (ITGP) is the world's leading publisher for governance and compliance. Our industry-leading pocket guides, books, training resources, and toolkits are written by real-world practitioners and thought leaders. They are used globally by audiences of all levels, from students to C-suite executives.

Our high-quality publications cover all IT governance, risk, and compliance frameworks, and are available in a range of formats. This ensures our customers can access the information they need in the way they need it.

Other publications that may be of interest include:

- *A Guide to Effective Internal Management System Audits – Implementing internal audits as a risk management tool* by Andrew W Nichols, *www.itgovernancepublishing.co.uk/product/a-guide-to-effective-internal-management-system-audits*
- *PRINCE2® in Action – Project management in real terms* by Susan Tuttle, *www.itgovernancepublishing.co.uk/product/prince2-in-action*
- *The PRINCE2 Agile® Practical Implementation Guide – Step-by-step advice for every project type, Second edition* by Jamie Lynn Cooke, *www.itgovernancepublishing.co.uk/product/the-prince2-agile-practical-implementation-guide-step-by-step-advice-for-every-project-type-second-edition*

For more information on ITGP and branded publishing services, and to view our full list of publications, visit *www.itgovernancepublishing.co.uk*.

To receive regular updates from ITGP, including information on new publications in your area(s) of interest, sign up for our newsletter at *www.itgovernancepublishing.co.uk/topic/newsletter*.

Branded publishing

Through our branded publishing service, you can customize ITGP publications with your organization's branding.

Find out more at *www.itgovernancepublishing.co.uk/topic/branded-publishing-services*.

Related services

ITGP is part of GRC International Group, which offers a comprehensive range of complementary products and services to help organizations meet their objectives.

For a full range of resources, visit *www.itgovernanceusa.com*.

Training services

The IT Governance training program is built on our extensive practical experience designing and implementing management systems based on ISO standards, best practice, and regulations.

Our courses help attendees develop practical skills and comply with contractual and regulatory requirements. They also support career development via recognized qualifications.

Learn more about our training courses and view the full course catalog at *www.itgovernanceusa.com/training*.

Professional services and consultancy

We are a leading global consultancy of IT governance, risk management, and compliance solutions. We advise organizations around the world on their most critical issues, and present cost-saving and risk-reducing solutions based on international best practice and frameworks.

We offer a wide range of delivery methods to suit all budgets, timescales, and preferred project approaches.

Find out how our consultancy services can help your organization at *www.itgovernanceusa.com/consulting*.

Industry news

Want to stay up to date with the latest developments and resources in the IT governance and compliance market? Subscribe to our Weekly Round-up newsletter and we will send you mobile-friendly emails with fresh news and features about your preferred areas of interest, as well as unmissable offers and free resources to help you successfully start your projects. *www.itgovernanceusa.com/weekly-round-up*.

Lightning Source UK Ltd.
Milton Keynes UK
UKHW020956061022
410026UK00011B/465

9 781787 783744